# THE BEST OF BROADWAY
# (AND BEYOND)

# THE BEST OF BROADWAY (AND BEYOND)

A 2026 REVIEW OF LAST YEAR'S STANDOUT SHOWS

BEST OF LIVE THEATRE SERIES

BRIAN GUY

PREVIEW NIGHT PRESS

Copyright © 2026 Brian Guy

All rights reserved.

No part of this book may be reproduced in any form or by any electronic or mechanical means, including information storage and retrieval systems, without written permission from the author, except for the use of brief quotations in a book review.

The opinions and impressions shared in this book are solely those of the author. They are based on personal knowledge, observation, and experience, and should not be interpreted as guarantees or formal recommendations. Individual experiences may vary.

eBook ISBN 979-8-9942273-9-8
Paperback ISBN 979-8-9942273-7-4
Hardcover ISBN 979-8-9942273-8-1
Large Print Edition ISBN 979-8-9949164-0-7

Published by Preview Night Press
Bainbridge Island, Washington

26021801

*For my Mom*

# CONTENTS

| | |
|---|---|
| 1. CURTAIN SPEECH | 1 |
| 2. THE WRITE-UP | 5 |
|   Broadway Musicals | 5 |
|     Hadestown | 5 |
|     Ragtime | 7 |
|     Cabaret at the Kit Kat Club | 8 |
|     Maybe Happy Ending | 12 |
|     Just In Time | 13 |
|     Sondheim's Old Friends | 16 |
|     Death Becomes Her | 17 |
|     Hell's Kitchen | 18 |
|     Operation Mincemeat | 21 |
|     SMASH | 22 |
|     Gypsy | 24 |
|   Broadway Institutions | 27 |
|     Hamilton | 27 |
|     Wicked | 31 |
|   Broadway Plays | 33 |
|     John Proctor is the Villain | 33 |
|     Purpose | 35 |
|     Liberation | 37 |
|     Punch | 39 |
|     Oh, Mary! | 40 |
|     Art | 42 |
|     Good Night, and Good Luck | 43 |
|   Off-Broadway Musicals | 44 |
|     Bat Boy: The Musical | 44 |
|     Mexodus | 49 |
|     JOY: A New True Musical | 50 |
|   Off-Broadway Plays | 52 |
|     Caroline | 52 |
|     Sexual Misconduct of the Middle Classes | 54 |

| | |
|---|---|
| KYOTO | 56 |
| Twelfth Night | 58 |
| Seattle Musicals | 59 |
|   Come From Away | 59 |
|   After Midnight | 63 |
| Seattle Plays | 66 |
|   Fancy Dancer | 66 |
|   The Play That Goes Wrong | 67 |
|   An Enemy of the People | 69 |
|   Dial M for Murder | 71 |
| **3. LOBBY TALK** | 73 |
| Quick Takes | 73 |
|   The Bridges of Madison County (Original Broadway Cast Reunion Concert) | 73 |
|   Beau the Musical | 74 |
|   Little Shop of Horrors | 75 |
|   Two Strangers (Carry A Cake Across New York) | 75 |
|   Gruesome Playground Injuries | 76 |
|   This World of Tomorrow | 77 |
| **4. BONUS CONTENT** | 79 |
| Community Theatre | 79 |
|   Sondheim Tribute Revue | 79 |
| High School Theatre | 81 |
|   Grease | 81 |
| **5. STAGE DOOR** | 83 |
| *About the Author* | 85 |
| *Also by Brian Guy* | 87 |
| *Preview Night Press* | 89 |

# 1

# CURTAIN SPEECH

Why in the world is there yet another Best of 2025 book? My theatre addiction required me to write this, but there are worse drugs. And hey, we need as much escape and distraction as we can get in current times.

What I hope to do with this book is praise and publicize some smaller shows that perhaps you haven't heard of, in addition to sending love to the obvious inclusions. Did you see *Caroline* by Preston Max Allen at MCC? If not, you need to read this book! Did you see *Beau the Musical* by Douglas Lyons and Ethan D. Pakchar? No? Well then read on!

There are also a couple of unusual choices I have made that make this book unique. For one, I am including some shows from the 2024-25 season (or older) that were still running in 2025. These are shows I did not get to see until 2025, so they are a part of my personal "Best of 2025." The table of contents will show you which specific shows I am covering.

I am also including a few shows from the Seattle area that were among my top favorites of the year. And just to be inclusive (and because hey it's my book, my rules), I'm even including a couple of amateur productions with volunteer actors: one from a community theatre and even one from a high school production. Why? This particular community theatre performance and this one high school production truly were two of my favorite experiences of the year (out of over 80 shows) and were more fun than some professional Broadway productions. Plus, how fun for a community theatre volunteer performer to get their name in a Broadway book? (I am leaving out the high school performer names, since many of them are minors). Differentiation, check.

The New York shows I cover are from six trips taken in June, July, September, October, November, and December. The record low trip was two shows in one day during a quick weekend trip, and the record high trip was 14 shows in seven days during a December trip.

Seeing 14 shows in seven days did not allow me to take as many notes as I normally would with a more reasonable one show per day schedule, so you will notice my comments about the shows I saw in December are much shorter. Therefore, please know the length of my write-up on a given show in no way reflects how much I enjoyed the show. If the show is in this book, then it means I really liked the show.

I have therefore divided this book into two sections: "The Write-Up" and "Lobby Talk." "The Write-Up" includes the shows where I have more to say, and "Lobby Talk" includes the shows where I have brief comments. There are shows in "Lobby Talk" that I liked more than some of the shows in "The Write-Up," and vice versa. The division is more about the length of my comments than it is about my ranking of the show.

As for how I sorted the shows, you can read a little bit into this (alphabetical is boring), but don't read too much into it. I might change the sort order depending on my mood on a given day or perhaps due to recency bias.

If you are hoping for some drama in this book about drama, I will disappoint you right now and tell you I am not writing about any of the shows I did not love. I don't want to spend time and energy writing about bad experiences, so this book is just about the good ones. This is a book of love. That said, if a show is missing, it does not mean I did not like it. It just means either I didn't see it or I didn't feel like writing about it for whatever reason. Or I wrote a lot about it, decided there was too much criticism in what I was saying, so cut it from the book. Again, this is a "why I love you" book, not a "why you bug me" book (some shows frustrate me).

Within "The Write-Up," I organize the book into these categories: Broadway Musicals, Broadway Institutions (*Hamilton* and *Wicked*), Broadway Plays, Off-Broadway Musicals, Off-Broadway Plays, Seattle Musicals, and Seattle Plays. Okay, curtain time! Please remember to turn off your phone (unless you're reading this book on it), and let's jump in!

## 2

## THE WRITE-UP

In this section, I am featuring the shows where I wrote more notes after the show and therefore have more to say. As a reminder, it does not necessarily mean I rank these shows higher than the ones mentioned in the later section, "Lobby Talk."

Also, as previously mentioned, read a little bit—but not too much—into how I have sorted the shows.

## BROADWAY MUSICALS

### Hadestown

Performances attended: Wednesday, July 16 and Sunday, December 14, 2025 at Walter Kerr Theatre

It does not happen very often, but every once in a while you think to yourself, "This is one of the best shows I have ever seen." *Hadestown* is one of the all-time best. It did win the Tony Award for "Best Musical" in 2019, and as of 2026, it is still running on Broadway seven years later, so others must agree with me.

*Hadestown* is the heartbreaking love story of Orpheus and Eurydice and also features Hades and Persephone. Even though many people know the ending, this production I saw was so good that there were screams in the audience, followed by crying. This show stays with you after you leave.

This New York production was significantly better than the tour, as the sound, lighting, set, and cast were phenomenal. This is one to see in New York. For example, on the Broadway stage, characters actually do transport underground via a trap door, which is not possible at many tour venues. This also makes for a much more dramatic ending (I do not recall the screams from the audience at the tour production).

The sound quality at Walter Kerr Theatre was excellent, and the sound engineering of *Hadestown* was among the best I have experienced. The lighting was also excellent in this show, and the set was impressive.

This show and this cast were as close to perfection as you can get. This was also true of the orchestra.

The cast I experienced in July included Ali Louis Bourzgui as Orpheus, Myra Molloy as Eurydice, Lana Gordon as Persephone, Phillip Boykin as Hades, and Daniel Breaker as Hermes. This cast, including The Fates and workers chorus, was one of the best casts I have seen on Broadway.

After my matinee of *Hadestown* ended, I walked to Sardi's to meet a friend for dinner. I fought tears the entire walk there.

I liked the show so much that I took my daughter to see it when we were in town in December. I had heard the buzz surrounding new-ish cast member Jack Wolfe's performance as Orpheus, but you have to see him in person to understand just how gifted he is as a performer.

What's funny about *Hadestown* is I had actually seen it before but didn't really remember it. I saw a national tour production in Seattle, but I had a very high up seat at that show and couldn't see well. By contrast, the Walter Kerr Theatre in

New York is small and intimate and provides a fantastic experience. My daughter asked if we could just see *Hadestown* every day of our trip instead of all the other shows. It is a show I hope to see again and again many more times, and I listen to the cast recording frequently.

## Ragtime

Performances attended: Friday, October 10 and Thursday, December 18, 2025 at Lincoln Center Theater at the Vivian Beaumont

"That was the best show I've ever seen," is what I frequently overheard and what I have seen written on message boards about this latest production of *Ragtime*. From the stunning costumes to the lighting design to the perfect sound and jaw-dropping vocals, this show was indeed momentous. The story is timely, and this musical from 1996 based on the 1975 novel hits hard in 2025-26.

This production of *Ragtime* ties with *Hadestown* for being my overall favorite musicals I experienced in 2025. This was also one of the shows I returned to see again in December, so my daughter could experience it.

This production was directed by Lear deBessonet. Everything about this production felt as close to perfection as you can get.

At my performance in October, we stopped the show multiple times for standing ovations (this did not happen in December). When this happened, it had only happened one other time for me in 2025, which was for Audra McDonald at the Saturday night performance of *Gypsy* the night before The Tony Awards. The third and final time this happened in a 2025 show was at *The Bridges of Madison County* Original Broadway Cast Reunion Concert, which I will discuss later in the book.

The standout performances were Nichelle Lewis as Sarah

and Joshua Henry as Coalhouse Walker, Jr. They each kept somehow taking their performances to the next level. Just when you thought they were peaking in a musical number, they then gave you even more.

In the original Broadway production of *Ragtime*, Audra McDonald won the Tony Award for "Best Performance by a Featured Actress in a Musical" for her portrayal of Sarah, and Brian Stokes Mitchell was nominated for the Tony Award for "Best Performance by a Leading Actor in a Musical." Fast forward to 2026, and Nichelle and Joshua will likely be contenders.

This entire cast was phenomenal, and everyone in this company should feel very proud both of their individual performances and for being a part of this magical production. The full list of the cast and creative team is available on Lincoln Center Theater's website.

Early in the show, one of the first impressions was the quality of the stunning costumes, designed by Linda Cho. These beautiful costumes of course also popped due to the exceptional lighting design by Adam Honoré. Kai Harada's sound design and James Moore's musical direction were perfect, and the sound engineering and sound levels were exactly as they should be. My pet peeve is sound engineers who ruin beautiful vocals with ridiculously high sound levels, and I so much appreciated the competence and quality of the sound engineering in this production.

I am thrilled I got to experience this show twice in 2025.

## Cabaret at the Kit Kat Club

Performance attended: Tuesday, September 9, 2025 at the Kit Kat Club at the August Wilson Theatre

*Cabaret* is a tough show to watch in current times. I admit to postponing seeing this show until later in 2025, to make sure I was emotionally ready. I originally scheduled it for October, but I continued to grow anxious the show would close early, as so many shows were doing in 2025.

When I received an alert that Billy Porter would be out for my October show, I pulled it forward to September, as I did want to see both Billy Porter and Marisha Wallace together. Then I got another alert that Billy would be out for my September date, and I was advised to reschedule for Billy's (then scheduled) return on Thursday, September 11. Based on what I knew about the situation, I thought (1) it seems unlikely Billy will actually be back on Thursday, and (2) do I really want to see him try to perform when he will likely still be recovering?

Literally the day before it was announced he was not returning and that the show would close early on September 21, I secured a seat for September 9. I feel so lucky I did so before the rush of folks rescheduling. While I was not able to get my dead center front row seat in Mezzanine 4 (the closer mezzanine), I was at least able to still get a front row seat in the same section, a bit off-center. I was far enough to the side that Marisha's first entrance caught me by surprise. Her very first entrance was to come into my row, and she stopped and sang directly to me, while I was standing to let her walk by in the tight row. Incredible.

The cast commented after the show what a great audience we were, as I suspect it may have been their first full house in a while. I had booked my seat not knowing if I would get Marty Lauter or David Merino as the Emcee, and I actually did not really care, as I had heard both of them were just so good. I did double check that Marisha would be performing at my show, as I did want to see her.

Before I talk more about the show, I want to first discuss the pre-show. I have come to very much appreciate when directors take the time to establish a vibe before the show even starts. In a Seattle production of *After Midnight*, discussed later in this book, the lighting design and view of the set had a significant impact on me when I first walked into the house, well before the show actually started. At *John Proctor is the Villain*, the loud pop music sets a mood before the show starts. In several shows, there is a show before the show happening on stage. It is always good to get to your seat early. In this production of *Cabaret*, the director starts setting the mood before you even enter the venue. This pre-show vibe matters and can greatly add to the experience.

Once inside, there was live entertainment in the basement as well as several bars. It was fun to walk around and explore. The vibe and mood were being set.

I see enough shows that I absolutely love it when something unique jumps out at me. This only happens in a subset of the shows I see. In this production, I was fairly quickly in awe of the emcee's stage makeup with this lighting design and on this set. It is hard to explain, but it triggered a unique emotional response. Kudos to the makeup design by Guy Common and the lighting design by Isabella Byrd. Guy and Isabella established my first impression once the show started, and this was truly exceptional work.

I also want to call out the sound design by Nick Lidster. I am picky about sound, and this was one of the best quality shows I have experienced for sound design. The acoustics in the venue were so good, and the orchestra placement also worked so well. My ears were very happy throughout this show.

My performance had quite a few understudies, and I do want to call them out, as they did such a great job. David Merino was listed as an understudy for the Emcee at my performance, perhaps simply because the Playbills were not updated, but let's just call them the lead now (along with Marty). They are so fantastic in this role. They were also a joy to meet after the show, as they are so kind and clearly having so much fun with their success in this show. They even photobombed my picture with Marisha.

Price Waldman filled in for Herr Schultz, Corinne Munsch filled in for Fritzie/Kost, Kayla Jenerson filled in for Rosie, Christian Kidd filled in for Lulu, and Karl Skyler Urban filled in for Herman/Train Officer/Max. Congrats to these performers for their great work! The regulars were also fantastic.

Marisha Wallace lived up to the hype, and her voice combined with the solid sound engineering made for such an enjoyable experience. This is a show I would have enjoyed seeing a second time, even though it is such a painful story. The rationalization would be to also see Marty, but my schedule unfortunately did not allow this.

I also really enjoyed the set, which is surprising to say given its simplicity. The experience was just so intimate and immersive, and the seating configuration was thoughtful and effective. I sat in the closer of the two mezzanines (a.k.a. the new mezzanine), and before the show, it felt odd seeing other audience members across from me in the other mezzanine, but once the show started, you could no longer see them. I love these non-traditional seating configurations. I did have a scare when I first sat down, in that a chandelier was dead center in my line of sight and blocked much of my view of the stage. Everyone around me was concerned about it. I went and asked the front of house staff about it, and they let me know the chandelier would be raised when the show started. I shared the good news with my seat neighbors, and we did a collective "phew!"

On one hand, I very much look forward to seeing *Cabaret* again one day. But on the other hand, how can it match the production quality of this presentation, especially since we now know the economics of this show just didn't work? I feel lucky I got to see such a deluxe production of this classic. It's such a heavy show that I actually now need a minute to recover just from writing about it. If you have seen *Cabaret* and have a similar trigger feeling after reliving it in your head just now, please feel free to take a moment before we jump into the next show.

## Maybe Happy Ending

Performances attended: Wednesday, June 11 and Saturday, December 20, 2025 at Belasco Theatre

I first saw this show in June during my Tony Awards trip, and then I saw it again in December with my daughter.

*Maybe Happy Ending* is the love story of two retired robots, each a different model with strengths and weaknesses the other does not possess, dealing with living life to its fullest while also aging. I get tired of saying a story "hits hard," but damn, I am aging, and the battery metaphor and the charger metaphor totally work for me.

It is also the joyful, heartwarming story that we all need right now. Add in excellent music, a great set and costumes, good lighting and sound design, and the excellent acting of Darren Criss and Helen J. Shen, and you have yourself a Tony Award-winning "Best Musical."

In early 2025, when I was planning my next trip to Broadway, *Maybe Happy Ending* was not even on my radar. I knew I wanted to see *Redwood* and *SMASH*, but that was about as far as I had gotten. Later, I was attending an Opening Night celebration for the play *Golden* at ACT Theatre in Seattle, when the topic came up with one of the theatre's interns. He told me, "You have to see *Maybe Happy Ending!*"

I went home, looked up the show, and immediately recognized Darren Criss. Whoa, how did I miss this show? As a fan of *Glee*, I thought how fun would it be to see Darren Criss back to back with Jonathan Groff (I had already booked *Just In Time* tickets by this point). I watched some clips from the show, and

Helen J. Shen's character was hilarious. I was now just as excited to see Helen as I was Darren.

The next surprise was to find out my daughter is a huge fan of Darren Criss, even though she had not watched *Glee*. "How do you know Darren?" I asked her. "Duh, he is totes lowkey rizz (or something like that) in *A Very Potter Musical*!"

This was my favorite show (musical or play) of all nine shows I saw during the June trip, and I agree with it winning the Tony Award for "Best Musical." I will also call out *Just In Time* for being my favorite experience of the trip. *Maybe Happy Ending* and *Just In Time* were the first two shows I decided my daughter needed to see during our December trip.

In this show, Darren Criss stood out for his physical acting, and Helen J. Shen stood out for her comedy and delivery. She was very funny in the shows I saw, and I am confident we will be seeing much more of her on stage in the future.

## Just In Time

Performances attended: Thursday, June 12 and Friday, December 19, 2025 at Circle in the Square

*Just In Time* was yet another one of a handful of shows I went back to in December, so that my daughter could also experience it. Immediately before *Just In Time*, we saw a matinee of *Beau the Musical* Off-Broadway, which I talk about later in this book, and it was a similar immersive experience in a nightclub setting. After seeing *Beau*, I thought to myself, oh no, I've ruined *Just In Time* for my daughter, because *Beau* provides the same immersive experience but in an even more intimate environment and with a deep story. "We are now headed to a similar show but in a bigger venue!" I worried. But as soon as the show started and as soon as Jonathan Groff entered, all those concerns immediately went away, because there is no other Jonathan Groff. His energy level and his presence were just magic. That said, I may have to go back and see *Just In Time* a third time, in order to see Jeremy Jordan in the role (Jeremy is announced to replace Jonathan).

*Just In Time* is the story of singer Bobby Darin, and the theatre is converted into an immersive nightclub. The cast was stacked with talent.

Thursday night, June 12, marked my ninth and final show of that Broadway trip. I was tired, but I was also very excited to see Jonathan Groff for the first time. I had heard COVID was going through some Broadway companies, so my first task was to make sure he was in the cast for the night. The front of house manager told me that so far, everyone was in for that night's show. Phew!

I had just been invited to Opening Night for *Call Me Izzy* that night, so if Jonathan was out, I needed to quickly get to Studio 54. Because *Call Me Izzy* was nearby and because it started one hour earlier than *Just In Time*, I did get to enjoy some of the Opening Night festivities outside the venue. I looked into rescheduling my *Just In Time* show, because Opening Nights are so fun, but I had reserved "banquette seating" on the floor, which was now sold out for quite some time. I decided to stick with *Just In Time* and see *Call Me Izzy* on a future trip (side note: *Call Me Izzy* was apparently very good, according to friends who went to Opening Night).

This was my first time attending a show at Circle in the Square, and I actually had a hard time finding it! I have never before had trouble finding a Broadway venue, because you can usually spot the show's signage from a block or more away. But as Jonathan Groff said, "Welcome to the show in *Wicked*'s basement!" So there is your clue: if you see signage for *Wicked* and are at the *Wicked* venue, you are very close. There just was not great signage for *Just In Time* on the *Wicked* side.

When the house opened, I walked in and immediately thought wow, this venue is much smaller than I expected! The smaller the better, so this was exciting. I was refused a Playbill, which confused me, and then it was explained to me that patrons on the floor would not get their Playbills until after the show. It makes sense, as the show is so immersive that we are sometimes part of the show. The Playbills would add clutter and distraction. Similarly, our complimentary beverage would also be collected prior to the show starting. That is right, there were nightclub servers offering a complimentary beverage. I was directed to a sofa immediately next to the second stage, and it was unlike any seat I have ever had at any prior show. I met my unplanned date for the show, a woman in town for business who purchased the other seat on our sofa. By traditional theatre seating standards, this sofa could possibly fit three patrons, so it was nice we were not squished in and had ample room on our sofa in what they called banquette seating.

I went back to take my daughter to the show in December, and she similarly loved it, even though we were exhausted from 14 shows in seven days. I purchased the same banquette sofa seats, except I flipped us to the other side, just so I could have a different perspective. She was thrilled when Jonathan looked her in the eye and sang to her.

You may hear theatre regulars talk about "getting to see the original cast" in a show, and this was definitely one where it was special to see this original cast, as this cast was just so good. It wasn't just Jonathan Groff but also Gracie Lawrence, Erika Henningsen, Michele Pawk, Emily Bergl, Joe Barbara, Lance Roberts, Caesar Samayoa, and more—too many to mention! The replacement cast members we experienced in December were also excellent. You could have a principal out and covered by an understudy, and you would still be at a show with a ridiculous number of top performers.

While the story is about Bobby Darin, you do not need to be a fan to enjoy this show. The story moves quickly, the music is fun, the energy is high, and what is special about this show is just how immersive it is. This show could be tricky to tour, due to the unique set, so this is one to prioritize seeing in New York.

Because of the smaller venue size, you need to plan in advance to see this show. While there likely is not a bad seat in the house, your risk is the show may be sold out when you are in town.

Now I admit I have been known to say this show does not work without Jonathan, and it will end when he leaves. I stand corrected. Jeremy Jordan has been announced as Jonathan's replacement, and now I want to go see the show again to see Jeremy.

## Sondheim's Old Friends

Performance attended: Saturday, June 7, 2025 at Manhattan Theatre Club at the Samuel J. Friedman Theatre

The Playbill for *Sondheim's Old Friends* adds the tagline, "A Great Big Broadway Show." Yes, it was! Calling it a Staged Concert just doesn't do it justice, and I felt like I was seeing so many mini-musicals in one shot. Mrs. Lovett even does her thing right there in front of us! And I am fairly picky when it comes to performances of "Agony," and many productions end up letting me down. Not this one. "Agony" was fantastic!

I had been to many Sondheim tribute concerts before, and I had a pretty long wish list of shows to see during this trip to New York City for the Tony Awards, so I was initially reluctant to add this concert to my schedule. I will confess it was Bernadette Peters and Lea Salonga who caught my attention. My surprise was that the entire cast was loaded with superstars, and this "concert" ended up being much more than just a concert, and every single cast member had impeccable vocals.

I grabbed a front row orchestra seat, hoping the stage wouldn't be too high and wondering how close I would be to Bernadette and Lea. This show was great for front row, as the stage was not too high at all, and the performers were just a few feet away when they came downstage. Bernadette and Lea were frequently all the way downstage, and I was treated to Bernadette singing directly to me—with eye contact—for much of the show.

This show was my first time seeing Bernadette perform, and I now get it why she is such a big deal. Of all the performers I have ever seen in my lifetime, she is up there as one of the best. There is just something about her presence that is unique, hypnotizing, and addictive. In case it is not clear, I really enjoyed this show.

An outstanding bucket list item I now have—because of this show—is to see Gavin Lee as Scar in *Disney's The Lion King* on Broadway. Gavin stood out to me in *Sondheim's Old Friends*, and it is now a high priority of mine to experience his Scar. I imagine he is going to be so scary, so evil, and I cannot wait to see his performance.

## Death Becomes Her

Performance attended: Saturday, September 6, 2025 at Lunt-Fontanne Theatre

*Death Becomes Her* is another show I will go see again in order to see Betsy Wolfe, who is replacing Megan Hilty. I loved Betsy in *& Juliet* and in *JOY*, which I write about in a bit, and I am excited to see her in *Death Becomes Her.*

I knew *Death Becomes Her* would be funny and a good time, but it very much exceeded my expectations across the board. The production quality was much higher than I expected. I had been trying to see this show since June 2025, but I very much wanted to see it with Megan Hilty, Jennifer Simard, Christopher Sieber, and Michelle Williams on the stage. Megan went out with her vocal injury the first time I tried to see it, and then I needed to prioritize other shows that were about to close.

What surprised me the most was the outstanding ensemble. Fantastic choreography was such a theme in 2025, and I do not always expect it in a comedy. Christopher Gattelli did such a nice job, and this was one of the better quality musicals I experienced in 2025.

There were so many highlights in this show, but I do not want to give away any spoilers. I knew a couple of spoilers going in, and I wish I did not.

I came into this show primarily just a fan of Megan Hilty, and I left this show also a new fan of Jennifer Simard, Christopher Sieber, and Michelle Williams. What a cast. The entire company was stellar.

On one hand, I feel like *Death Becomes Her* is underrated and a sleeper, but on the other hand, it is in a very small group of shows still open, as of 2026. This is one that will exceed your expectations.

## Hell's Kitchen

Performance attended: Thursday, July 17, 2025 at Sam S. Shubert Theatre

I had been (wrongly) content to wait and see the national tour of *Hell's Kitchen* in Seattle in July 2026. I had my tickets. But then Christopher Jackson joined the cast, so I decided to go ahead and see it in New York. That was the right call, as I absolutely loved this production in New York. While we can expect the tour will be good, it cannot duplicate this cast, this sound quality, this set, and this lighting, all of which contributed to the show's experience.

I was especially struck by the dancing, which when combined with the costumes, lighting, orchestra, and this cast's vocals and acting, made for a powerful experience. I also liked the balance of projections and traditional set pieces. The set was stunning. The sound engineering was excellent.

The story includes the difficulty of parenting a teenager as a single parent and the challenges of growing up in New York City at the time. The story is inspired by and loosely based on the life of Alicia Keys.

At my performance, Ali was played by understudy Lulu Oro Hamlett, and I did not realize she was an understudy until after the show. What I really liked about Lulu's performance was that she was not only a fantastic singer and dancer, but she also possessed excellent acting skills. Her emotions came through both when she was singing and speaking, and she was always present. This is not always the case with Broadway performers, as it is exhausting work. I noticed and appreciated Lulu's presence and energy. It was surprising to me to learn this show was her Broadway debut. Lulu has a bright future ahead of her.

Kecia Lewis as Miss Liza Jane was my favorite performance in the show, and it is no surprise to me she won the Tony Award for "Best Performance by an Actress in a Featured Role in a Musical" for this role (she was in the original cast).

I also very much liked Lamont Walker II's performance as Knuck. His vocals were incredible, and his acting was also top notch. Do you see a theme here? I recognized Lamont and was trying to figure out where I have seen him before. I now know he was in the original cast of *MJ*, which I saw with its Original Broadway Cast in 2022. Lamont was in the original cast of *Hell's Kitchen* as Riq.

Jessica Vosk played Ali's mother, Jersey. She, too, had both incredible vocals and acting skills, and the audience felt her emotions. She has previously played Elphaba in *Wicked*. Jessica had some great lines in the show, and she made me tear up more than once.

We do not see much of Christopher Jackson until Act 2. When I watched *Hamilton* on Disney+ the day it came out, and then again later that night as a part of Lin-Manuel Miranda's online watch party, one word came to mind to describe Christopher Jackson's vocals: butter. To this day, I refer to his buttery voice. He has one of the most beautiful male voices I have ever heard. While his vocals sound similar in *Hamilton* and in *Hell's Kitchen*, his characters are very different. In *Hamilton*, he does a great job presenting us with a stressed out and exhausted George Washington. In *Hell's Kitchen*, his character is much more cheery, and it is fun to see a skilled actor perform such different characters. Despite my very high expectations, Christopher Jackson exceeded those expectations with his performance in *Hell's Kitchen*.

The ensemble in this show really stood out, too, as the choreography, dancing, and singing truly were top notch. The set and lighting added to the experience, as previously mentioned.

Angela Birchett, Nyseli Vega (original Broadway cast), Chad Carstarphen (original cast), Mykhel Duckett, Jackie Leon (original cast), Oscar Whitney, Jr., Jakeim Hart (original cast), all of the dance ensemble, and any other cast members I did not specifically mention were fantastic. This cast was well balanced, and what a treat to still have so many members of the original cast.

Two comments about the venue: the stage was a bit higher than other NYC venues, so front row orchestra was a bit less optimal than at other shows. I recommend sitting a bit farther back or sitting in the front row of the mezzanine. That said, front row orchestra was very fun at this show, despite the non-optimal view. The second comment is that this show was loud. The loudness did not bother me, as the sound quality was excellent, but consider bringing ear protection if you are sensitive to loud shows.

Do see this show in New York if you can, even though it is on tour.

I am still conflicted about seeing the national tour production versus just keeping my memory of the Broadway production. I did enjoy the recent national tour productions of both *Shucked* and *& Juliet*, despite having seen them both on Broadway with their original casts, so I am leaning towards seeing it on tour.

If you listen to the cast recording and enjoy the music, I feel like you will absolutely love this show. If you tend to hate jukebox musicals, then perhaps skip this one.

## Operation Mincemeat

Performance attended: Wednesday, July 16, 2025 at Golden Theatre

*Operation Mincemeat* is the true story about how Great Britain fooled the Germans in World War II by having fake invasion papers in the suitcase of a corpse posing as a dead soldier. This was a history lesson but in the form of a very fun musical. What made this show work was the incredibly talented cast, the good music, and the very funny script.

While Jak Malone won the Tony Award for "Best Performance by an Actor in a Featured Role in a Musical," this entire cast was excellent. My performance had understudy Gerianne Pérez, who you may have previously seen in the national tour of *SIX*, fill in for Ewen Montagu and others, and patrons sitting around me agreed Gerianne was one of our favorite performers in the show (we loved them all).

You could tell this cast had been performing together for a while, as there was so much chemistry within this cast, and they worked so well together. David Cumming, Claire-Marie Hall, Gerianne Pérez, Jak Malone, and Zoë Roberts were each exceptional despite playing so many characters!

The set was fairly simple in this show, and the music was a lot of fun. One tip is do not be late coming back from intermission, as the top of Act 2 was absolutely hilarious and not something you want to miss.

I will add this is a good one to listen to the cast recording ahead of time.

## SMASH

Performance attended: Friday, June 6, 2025 at Imperial Theatre

Oh *SMASH*. Hear me out on this one, as I know it had issues. Try not to judge me for loving it. There may be a small amount of bias, as this was the first show I saw in New York in 2025, so I had not yet experienced all the other incredible shows I would later see. Also, I had been warned on the message boards that it was very different from the TV show (which I had just binged in preparation), so my expectations were set.

*SMASH* is about the making of a musical about Marilyn Monroe. This Broadway version is fairly different from the TV series. Karen is a minor character and is Ivy's understudy. The director character is a gay man, which is again very different from the TV show. If you can go into the Broadway show knowing it is a different story with different characters, then you can love both. Too many patrons apparently could not do this, causing the show to close early.

When I was planning my trip to the Tony Awards in 2025, *SMASH* was the second show I booked (*Redwood* was the first), and *SMASH* was the first of nine shows I experienced during this trip. I had binge watched the TV series in early 2025 to prepare for the show, but watching the TV series first was certainly not a requirement. The Broadway production changes the story and some of the characters quite a bit. You can watch the TV series before or after the Broadway musical. They are both very enjoyable, even though they are different. I am aware some fans of the TV series were upset with the changes, and perhaps I am in the minority for enjoying both versions.

I saw *SMASH* on the Friday night of the Tony Awards weekend, so it was an energetic audience. I was most looking forward to seeing Brooks Ashmanskas, as I was familiar with his work in *The Prom*. I was also very excited to see John Behlmann, who I briefly met after *Shucked* on its Tony Awards Eve performance in 2023. I also watched John's vlog, *Jerry Duty*, prior to my trip, and I found it to be a fun behind the scenes look at the show.

For this show, I chose front row center mezzanine, which was a great choice to enjoy the spectacular choreography. I had been cheering for this nominated show to win the Tony Award for "Best Choreography."

I walked into Imperial Theatre on Friday night and saw the notice, "The role of Nigel will be played by McGee Maddox." Wait, isn't Nigel the character that Brooks plays? I checked my Playbill, and sure enough, Brooks called out for my performance. This was a big disappointment, but at least the other big names were still in the lineup. This is a risk of seeing a show right before or after The Tony Awards. Audra McDonald was apparently out at her Tony Awards Eve matinee performance of *Gypsy*, and Nicole Scherzinger was apparently out at her Tony Awards Eve evening performance of *Sunset Blvd*. Nicole was also out at my Wednesday evening performance of *Sunset Blvd.* following the Tony Awards.

From the start of the show, you fairly quickly got to experience amazing vocals, and the choreography was top notch. Experiencing Robyn Hurder singing and dancing while being thrown into the air was impressive. How does she do this? Hard work.

I came into this show not knowing much about Robyn Hurder and being more excited to see Brooks, Krysta Rodriguez, and John, and I left this show being a new fan of Robyn. She blew away my expectations. The entire cast was fantastic, and McGee Maddox did a great job covering for Brooks.

The reality in a highly competitive season is that Tony Awards matter, and I am disappointed that *SMASH* announced its closing after not winning its nominations. I am thrilled I got to experience this incredible show before it closed, whereas my *Redwood* performance was canceled and refunded after not receiving any Tony nominations.

What makes me most sad about *SMASH* is it is likely a show nobody will ever be able to see ever again. I wish every show would have a recording like *Hamilton* or *Merrily We Roll Along*, so that folks who miss the short run can still see it via streaming later.

## Gypsy

Performance attended: Saturday, June 7, 2025 at Majestic Theatre

*Gypsy* was not a show I was super excited to see again, but of course I had to see Audra McDonald. I scheduled this show for Tony Eve, the night before the Tony Awards, and it was therefore a very special audience.

*Gypsy* is the story of a stage mother who pushes her daughters hard, partially because she felt like she was never pushed by her mother. She believes they can become successful if she keeps on them.

I had originally booked *Redwood* as my show for the special slot of the Saturday evening show prior to the Tony Awards. In 2023, I had seen *Shucked* in this slot, and it was such a fun experience. It was also very impressive how quickly the company started moving set pieces into a moving truck immediately after the show, in order to take part of the set to the United Palace in Washington Heights for their Tony Awards performance that year. Tony Eve shows are fun.

Back when I first started organizing this trip, the two shows I was most excited to see were *Redwood* and *SMASH*, which I booked to be my Friday night show (I also snuck in *Sondheim's Old Friends* for a Saturday matinee).

I was of course so disappointed when *Redwood* got canceled, after not receiving any Tony Award nominations, and I began looking at my show schedule to see what shows from the following week I could move up to this special Saturday night slot. I am a seat snob, so I also needed a show that had at least as good of a seat open for this Saturday night show as what I already had booked. I also realized the box office likely wasn't going to help me unless my new seat cost at least as much as the seat I was asking to move. There was significant buzz around Audra McDonald's performance in *Gypsy*, and I did find a front row center mezzanine seat available. I called up the box office and asked if I could move my seat to the Saturday night show, and they helped me out.

Front row mezzanine at Majestic Theatre is not perfect, as there is a safety rail that blocks the view of anything happening downstage. This meant that periodically, all of us in the front row would lean forward to see downstage activity. This was rare enough that it did not bother us, and it gave us something to laugh about at intermission. I do, however, wonder if it was annoying to the patrons in the second and third rows of the mezzanine that we all kept leaning way forward in our seats several times throughout the show. If I had to do it over again, I would still likely book front row center mezzanine, as it does give you the best overall view of the musical, and you eliminate the risk of a tall person sitting in front of you.

For musicals, I tend to do either this seat or an aisle on one of the sides of Orchestra seating, since that aisle in the side section gives you a diagonal unobstructed view to the stage, even if there is a tall person in front of you. I find that too often the center orchestra section just does not have enough elevation from row to row, and you are in bad shape if a tall person sits in front of you. I talk at length about seat selection in my book, *Broadway for Beginners*.

The risk of seeing a show immediately before the Tony Awards is that your star may call out. This might be due to a conflict with a Tony Award performance rehearsal, or the star might just be exhausted. Performing eight shows over six days every week is exhausting enough, but now the actor has to deal with media, promotions, and just the nerves and excitement of Tony Award nominations.

Saying my expectations were high would be an understatement; I was about to see a legend perform. Audra and the rest of the cast delivered. One thing I was not expecting was just how incredible this audience was. The energy level was through the roof, and we caused the show to run for over three hours! The show is supposed to be 2 hours and 40 minutes long, which means we added a full 20 minutes of additional applause and standing ovations. This was one of only three shows in 2025 where we interrupted the show with standing ovations. The other two were *Ragtime* and *The Bridges of Madison County* Original Broadway Cast Reunion Concert.

Just the audience experience itself was a special experience most of us in this audience will never forget. The only somewhat similar experience for me was Cole Escola's performance in *Oh, Mary!* on Monday night, the first show after winning their Tony Award. That audience was also special.

Experiencing Audra and this cast was a bucket list item, and I will always treasure getting to see Audra perform in this show and with this special audience.

I need to specifically call out Audra's performances at the end of each act, as these were next level—beyond what you expect even of Audra. While Audra was fantastic throughout the show, her performances at the end of Act 1 and again at the end of Act 2 were performances you only get to experience maybe a few times in your life. They were jaw-dropping, heart-stopping, tear-invoking performances that only a great can do, and dare I say it was life changing to experience these performances firsthand. It was the type of performance that reminds any other actor in the audience, "yes, this is why I do this work and what I aspire to be." She gave it her all and put so much into this performance.

While her performance Sunday night at the Tony Awards (which I also saw live) was excellent, her performance the night before was even stronger, aided by being in the context of the story versus a standalone musical number Sunday night.

At the performance I attended, I also felt like Danny Burstein was a standout. The entire cast was excellent, and it was adorable watching one of the child performers sign autographs after the show. She was proud of her performance, as she should be.

# BROADWAY INSTITUTIONS

While I have seen both *Hamilton* and *Wicked* several times, the year 2025 was actually the first time I saw them on Broadway. They were indeed highlights of my 2025, so they made the cut for this book.

## Hamilton

Performance attended: Tuesday, July 15, 2025 at Richard Rodgers Theatre

*Hamilton* is about so much more than just Alexander Hamilton's life (or should I say Eliza Hamilton's life?). Ten years later, this show still delivers. This was only my fourth time seeing *Hamilton* live, and it was my first time seeing it in New York. It was actually not on my radar to see it in New York, as I have seen it so many times on Disney+, but multiple friends told me, "you must see it at the venue where it all started."

Okay, technically that would be Off-Broadway at The Public Theater, but we will let that detail slide and consider Richard Rodgers Theatre to be the room where it happened!

The first time I saw *Hamilton* was the national tour in Seattle in early 2018. It was an experience my family will not forget. In 2020, I was beyond excited for the Disney+ premiere to launch, and I watched it at least twice that day, including as a part of Lin-Manuel Miranda's online watch party. Even though it was on TV and not live, wow, this original cast was so good. I have no idea how many times I have watched *Hamilton* on Disney+ or have listened to the original cast recording. Many times.

In August 2022, I would see the national tour a second time, also in Seattle, and to my surprise, I did not love this production. It is possible I had too high of expectations after watching the original cast.

Therefore, when I saw the national tour in Seattle a third time, in February 2025, I lowered my expectations, and I made sure I did not watch the Disney+ version soon before the show. I walked into the theatre, and I actually teared up seeing the set. I suspect it is because of just how emotional of a time it was in 2020 when this show was a rare bright spot. I absolutely loved the cast and the performance in Seattle earlier in 2025.

I also was so fortunate to experience the original cast performing live at The Tony Awards in June, and this was one of my favorite moments of the evening. What a treat.

At this performance at Richard Rodgers Theatre, I was surrounded by people who had never seen the show live before, and this was their first time ever seeing it except for on Disney+. This created an exciting experience for everyone.

Before I get into the cast, I want to first comment about the lighting, costumes, and choreography. When the show started, the first thing I noticed was the beautiful costumes, which does not really make sense, since I had just seen the show in

February. I assume the national tour costumes are similar, so why did they jump out at me? What I concluded was that it was because the lighting was so much better in the Broadway production that it made the incredible costumes pop even more. I really enjoyed the lighting, and I have never before really noticed the lighting in the national tour of *Hamilton* (except for when King George changes the color). If someone asks me why to see *Hamilton* on Broadway, I would mention the lighting.

Next was the choreography, which seemed so much better to me than in the tour. After the show, I asked a cast member if the tour choreography is the same or different, and she said, "it is *supposed* to be the same." It is possible my reaction was again influenced by the lighting or maybe even by the venue. I really liked the choreography.

I browsed through the cast list and noticed that at my show, Aaron Burr, sir, would be played by understudy Alex Nicholson, whose bio states he was the standby in the national tour and primarily in the ensemble. Alex was actually the understudy for multiple principal characters, which always impresses me. It is hard enough to learn one character let alone several. Since I have never seen Leslie Odom, Jr. perform live in the role, I can say Alex is the best Aaron Burr, sir, I have seen. I really enjoyed his performance.

Another very important role in the show is King George, and perhaps no other role has such high expectations from the audience to deliver comedy. Similarly, because I have never seen Jonathan Groff in the role live, I can also say Jarrod Spector is the best King George I have ever seen. The crowd seemed to love him. Jarrod was excellent in the role and was so funny. He also had outstanding vocals. For readers in Seattle, you might recognize his name. Jarrod played Steven Spielberg in the 2022 World Premiere of *Bruce* at Seattle Rep.

Bryson Bruce was the next standout in his roles as Marquis

de Lafayette and Thomas Jefferson. The latter character was of course the crowd favorite, and Bryson definitely brought the thunder. One thing I noticed that was different from the prior performances I have seen is that Thomas Jefferson and James Madison, played by Ebrin R. Stanley (who also played Hercules Mulligan), had so much chemistry and friendship. The relationship between Jefferson and Madison was one of my favorite parts of the performance. Their synergy was outstanding, and their stage chemistry worked really well. Ebrin was therefore also a standout performer for me in the performance I saw. Bryson and Ebrin have raised the bar for what I will now look for in the friendship between Jefferson and Madison.

The casting of Tamar Greene as George Washington really worked for me, and his booming yet beautiful voice made so much sense for George Washington. He's a very different GW than the OG Christopher Jackson, and they both work very well, just in different ways. The way Tamar projected in certain parts of his songs was really powerful. Because I was seeing Christopher Jackson in *Hell's Kitchen* during the same week, I was actually a bit anxious about how I would react to George Washington, as I am a huge Christopher Jackson fan.

Samuel Seabury is a character's name I had to look up, because this was the first time I have ever thought of this character. This performance by Thayne Jasperson was the first time I have ever seen this character get so many laughs. Thayne had really developed this character, and it was so good. Thayne made an otherwise entertaining scene even better and very funny. Perhaps because it was unexpected, it was one of the funnier moments of Act 1. I really enjoyed Thayne's acting.

Last but not least, Trey Curtis was excellent as Alexander Hamilton, Alexander Ferguson did great as Phillip Schuyler and other characters, JJ Niemann was a fantastic Charles Lee, and I enjoyed the performances of Stephanie Umoh (Angelica), Morgan Anita Wood (Eliza), Cherry Torres (Peggy and Maria), and the rest of this cast. Anyone I did not specifically mention also did a solid job, as there were no weak performers in this show. I also want to again emphasize just how good this ensemble was, and I found myself frequently watching the dancers, which was yet another perk of watching the show live instead of on TV.

The show has aged well, and it was still a great time ten years later. And yes, it is definitely worth seeing in New York even if you have already seen the tour.

## Wicked

Performance attended: Friday, July 18, 2025 at Gershwin Theatre

This was my seventh time seeing *Wicked* but my first time seeing it on Broadway. I saw it for the first time in 2007 at the Hollywood Pantages, then I did not see it again until the national tour came to Seattle in 2019. I then saw it three more times when the national tour was in Seattle in 2024. My sixth time was just a few weeks earlier when the national tour was in Indianapolis.

The national tour performances were so good—this has been one of the better quality national tours—that I had been curious how the show on Broadway would compare.

Without giving spoilers, I will just say there were numerous enhancements in the experience in New York, and given the choice, it is definitely advantageous to see the show on Broadway. That said, the current national tour was very good. For comparison, the *Hamilton* national tour has been fairly similar to *Hamilton* on Broadway (I primarily noticed better lighting on Broadway), but *Wicked* seems more enhanced on Broadway.

The Gershwin Theatre is a large theatre (the largest Broadway theatre), so you do not get the typical Broadway intimacy you get at other venues, but it is still smaller than many tour venues. For example, the Gershwin Theatre seats 1933 patrons for *Wicked* on Broadway, while the Paramount Theatre in Seattle seats 2807 patrons. But *Hadestown* on Broadway at the Walter Kerr Theatre seats just 975 patrons. *Just In Time* seats just 690 patrons at Circle in the Square Theatre. These are large differences. Consider the size when you are selecting your seat. Unlike the national tour, where I recommended the mezzanine, up close in orchestra is very fun at this show on Broadway.

When you are at the Gershwin Theatre, you do feel a bit like you are in Oz. There is green carpeting at the entrance, green themes everywhere, and they have done a nice job with the branding. It is a nice venue.

Sometimes when you are seeing an older show, the cast can be inconsistent, and some performers might be great singers but not the best actors. At *Wicked*, despite the show's age, this cast was consistently excellent. Even though this was the seventh time I had seen *Wicked*, this might have been the first time when I left thinking both Glinda and Elphaba were equally outstanding throughout the entire show. Usually, one stands out over the other, either for the entire show or for one of the acts. It can flip from night to night even with the exact same cast (everyone has their great nights and their just good nights).

My show's excellent Elphaba was played by Lencia Kebede, and the excellent Glinda was played by Allie Trimm. They were not just good individually, but they also had good stage chemistry together.

There were three understudies in my show. Christianne Tisdale covered Madame Morrible, David Scott Purdy played the Witch's Father and the Ozian Official, and Micaela Martinez played the role of the midwife. This was the first time I have noticed the characters referred to as "Witch's Father" and "Ozian Official." It took me a minute to understand why, and it would be a spoiler to explain the reason. These understudies performed flawlessly, and I did not know they were understudies until I looked at the Playbill later after the show.

Jenna Bainbridge was so good as Nessarose, and it was the best performance I have ever seen of this character really portraying the evil later in the show. It was excellent acting showing us how the character evolved over time. Her brief moment of showing us the evil in Act 2 was a standout moment in the show for me.

Daniel Quadrino was also the best Boq I have ever seen, and he similarly had excellent acting expressing his emotions.

Jordan Litz as Fiyero was excellent casting and I also very much enjoyed his performance.

William Youmans as Doctor Dillamond was also excellent.

David Scott Purdy was outstanding, and at times I felt like I was listening to Joel Gray. I never got to see Joel in the role, but I listen to his vocals all the time on the cast recording.

Christianne Tisdale was the best Madame Morrible I have seen on stage, and similar to Jenna, she did such a good job portraying her evil.

The flying monkeys were also so much more present for me in this Broadway production versus the national tours. How scary that one was flying right over me! They all did a great job.

This entire cast and ensemble were consistently excellent across the board. The production was high quality.

If you are not able to see the show on Broadway, the national tour is also very good. But see it in New York if you can!

## BROADWAY PLAYS

### John Proctor is the Villain

Performance attended: Saturday, September 6, 2025 at Booth Theatre

*John Proctor is the Villain* is one of the all-time greatest plays. It is powerful, it is timely, and it is important. This production on Broadway was an example of a director taking a near perfect play from a skilled playwright and then making it even better. I will now be sure to look for other works by playwright Kimberly Belflower and by director Danya Taymor.

This is a play I unsuccessfully tried to squeeze in during my June and July trips to New York, and I am so happy I was able to see it during this closing weekend.

There is much to unpack in this story. This story covers many themes. My performance included all of the original Broadway cast members except for the character Shelby Holcomb, who was now played by Chiara Aurelia instead of Sadie Sink. While I was disappointed to not see the show earlier in its run with Sadie, Chiara's performance was outstanding. This show has excellent casting.

Nihar Duvvuri, Gabriel Ebert, Molly Griggs, Maggie Kuntz, Hagan Oliveras, Morgan Scott, Fina Strazza, and Amalia Yoo were the other cast members. They were each equally excellent in their roles.

One of the details I noticed in the set design was the level of detail in the hallway outside of the classroom. I only got to see glimpses of the hallway for a few seconds whenever the classroom door was opened, and there was more detail than I could take in during just those few seconds, but it did add to the experience. Similarly, on the opposite side, there was an outdoor space visible through a window. While perhaps not required, the outdoor space near stage right and the hallway near stage left made the set feel more complete than had it simply been just the classroom. It will be interesting to see if future productions add this impactful level of detail.

I also liked how the lighting design and sound design worked together at the end of each scene and throughout the show. And speaking of sound design, the pre-show music and playlist helped set the vibe and the setting, and I am very much a fan of shows creating the vibe before the show even starts. In other words, when done right, the show absolutely does start as soon as the house opens. Good shows do this well.

Every component of this production was excellent, and I am again just so happy I was able to see it during its closing weekend.

This important play should now be available for local theatres to program and produce, so please encourage your local theatre to do so! I will be seeing this play again every chance I get, and I also purchased a copy of the script for my daughter.

## Purpose

Performance attended: Sunday, July 13, 2025 at The Hayes Theater

*Purpose* was where I discovered Kara Young, who I will be talking about again later in this book, and I accidentally bought a ticket for what would be LaTanya Richardson Jackson's final performance in the cast!

*Purpose* is largely a family dinner table conversation, except this family is famous, and a star-struck guest has joined for dinner. What could go wrong? While the play is very, very funny, it is not just a comedy. This play touches on numerous timely topics that are hot topics when around a multi-generational dinner table where outside appearances matter greatly to them. Never mind any hypocrisy. I will avoid further plot discussion in order to prevent spoilers.

There was significant buzz in the audience, and this was not just because LaTanya Richardson Jackson's husband was in the house. This was her night. Samuel L. Jackson was in the house to support his wife's final performance in the show, which won the Tony Award for "Best Play." LaTanya was nominated for

"Best Performance by a Leading Actress in a Play," and it showed. She was just fantastic and was all the things you hope for in this Claudine character. I will be thinking about her performance for a while.

When I put this show on the calendar, I did not know it would be LaTanya's last performance, and it was a treat to see her perform and to attend this special show with her final performance. She was clearly a core reason this show won "Best Play."

Similarly, Kara Young as Aziza Houston provided one of the best performances you can experience on Broadway. Kara won the Tony Award for "Best Featured Actress in a Play." Her character provided much of the comic relief, but she also contributed to many of the important social messages in this story.

One of the discussion points after this show was just how outstanding the entire cast was. They worked so well together. If there was a standout, it was all of them together as one ensemble. Both Jon Michael Hill and Harry Lennix also received Tony Award nominations for "Best Leading Actor in a Play," and Glenn Davis received a Tony Award nomination for "Best Featured Actor in a Play." Alana Arenas also provided an incredible performance.

I very much liked the set, and the upstage window with the snowfall was especially thoughtful. It was fun to watch the snowfall change in intensity throughout the show. For non-theatre readers, the term upstage refers to the back of the stage away from the audience, versus downstage, which is closest to the audience. The lighting was minimal but effective, and the sound was enjoyable, since it did not feel like microphones were in use. I do not always like a play having a narrator, but it seemed to work well in this show. I liked how the lighting adjusted during moments of narration.

This show covered quite a few more social issues than I

expected, and I will leave out the details, since I enjoyed being surprised. No spoilers. There is likely at least one issue for everyone that will hit you and cause you to tear up, but fear not, as there is significant comic relief. The show was very, very funny while also addressing numerous timely issues.

Some of us were talking after the show about how a comedy with no social messages can be a lost opportunity, while a story with social issues but no comedy can be difficult. There is nothing wrong with a pure comedy, as it is important to also just have comic escape, but it is special to be treated to a show like this one where you get both. This show was just the right balance of addressing numerous social issues while also having more comedy than you expect.

I especially appreciated the story touching on neurodiversity and including neurodivergent characters. There were some absolutely beautiful monologues on this topic in Act 2.

To prevent spoilers, I will not describe one of my favorite moments of the show, but it is a moment of brilliant timing of comedy and drama happening at the same time, and the audience reaction was priceless. I do not think I have ever had this experience with an audience before, and it was timed perfectly. There was much brilliance in the writing, directing, and acting in this production.

## Liberation

Performance attended: Wednesday, October 8, 2025 at James Earl Jones Theatre

I was lucky enough to attend First Preview of the Broadway transfer of *Liberation* back in October at the James Earl Jones Theatre (for more explanation of the terms First Preview, previews, Opening Night, etc., see my *Broadway for Beginners* book). First Preview is an exciting experience, you sometimes get a gift, and much of the audience can be made up of producers, investors, and friends and family of the cast and creative team.

Because only the venue was new (this production had previously been running Off-Broadway), the show was already quite polished. *Liberation* is written by Bess Wohl and directed by Whitney White.

*Liberation* asks the question, what if you could talk to your deceased mother today and ask her questions about choices she made during her lifetime. Does she have any regrets? Would she do anything differently? In this case, a young woman figuring out her own life wants to know why did her feminist mother get married and have kids, and does she regret having her? Why did she seemingly stop her work around women's liberation?

To find out, the daughter takes us back to the 1970s, where we meet her mother and other women fighting for equality. There was a good mix of laughing and tearing up as we re-lived the 1970s, while at the same time assessing the current situation in 2025-26.

While the story is largely about challenges women uniquely face, it also dives into parenthood, work/life balance, marriage, relationships, and other complexities of life.

*Liberation* is a powerful story with exceptional performers. This production was high quality across the board.

The cast when I attended included Betsy Aidem, Audrey Corsa, Kayla Davion, Susannah Flood, Kristolyn Lloyd, Irene Sofia Lucio, Charlie Thurston, Adina Verson, Britt Faulkner, LeeAnne Hutchinson, Matt E. Russell, and Kedren Spencer.

I expect to see multiple Tony Award nominations for this excellent production, now that it has transferred to Broadway.

## Punch

Performance attended: Wednesday, September 10, 2025 at Manhattan Theatre Club at the Samuel J. Friedman Theatre

*Punch* is a new play by James Graham and directed by Adam Penford which played at the Samuel J. Friedman Theatre on Broadway.

This play is based on the book *Right from Wrong* by Jacob Dunne, which is based on a true story. *Punch* is about empathy, healing, forgiveness, and more. The story is both heartbreaking and heartwarming, and one goal of the story is to generate awareness from a tragedy. The story covers multiple timely themes.

I was on the fence about seeing this show, but early reviews were overall positive. In the end, I decided to trust the folks who are doing the Manhattan Theatre Club programming. They had not let me down before, and I had just been at this same venue back in June for *Sondheim's Old Friends*, which was one of my favorite productions of 2025.

With this play, MTC earned even more of my trust, and I will trust and prioritize MTC productions even more in the future. *Punch* was fantastic.

I was surprised to read that this show was Will Harrison's Broadway debut, as I felt like he had a standout performance. He played the lead character Jacob, and I very much enjoyed watching Will evolve his character over the course of the play. Will's performance was truly exceptional, and I loved the choices that were made by director Adam Penford and Will.

I knew coming in that Victoria Clark would be excellent (she was), and the fun surprise was that she played multiple characters who were very different from each other. It was also fun to hear the audience buzz during intermission as many of the patrons finally started to figure out why they recognized Victoria. I kept hearing, "That's Kimberly Akimbo!" I let it slide and did not correct them that she was actually Kimberly Levaco. Details.

Sam Robards was also fantastic in this play.

The entire cast was a joy to watch, and they were very polished and prepared given the show was still in previews when I saw it.

I also very much enjoyed the lighting design, sound design, and costumes. The simple set also worked well. The lighting and sound especially worked well together, which is always nice to see (and hear).

Neurodiversity was also a theme in the show. And the story was at least as heartwarming as it was heartbreaking. The characters in this story are all truly remarkable humans, and their empathy sets an example for all of us. And in this production, these incredible humans were played by top notch actors under great direction.

I ended up watching *Punch* a second time from home, via a livestream option. The livestream experience was very good.

## Oh, Mary!

Performance attended: Monday, June 9, 2025 at Lyceum Theatre
Oh, Cole!

This play asks the question what if Abraham Lincoln's death actually was not bad for Mary Todd Lincoln? *Oh, Mary!* is non-stop laughs and a fun show.

Do you know what was better than seeing this hilarious play that had all the buzz on Broadway? The answer is of course seeing that play at its very first performance after winning two Tony Awards. Cole Escola won the Tony Award for "Best Performance by an Actor in a Leading Role in a Play," and Sam Pinkleton won the Tony Award for "Best Direction of a Play." It was such an honor to meet both Cole and Sam after the show.

It is hard for me to understand how Cole could get on stage and perform that Monday night, less than 24 hours after winning their Tony Award. There may indeed have been a few moments of improv in that Monday night performance, and the crowd ate it up.

The energetic audience, sharing in the celebration knowing that this was such a special night and a special performance, made a very fun show even more fun.

At this performance, our Playbill included an insert with this message: "At this performance, the role of Mary's Husband will be played by Julian Manjerico." In case you read too quickly, the character is called "Mary's Husband." It is not Abraham Lincoln. This is just one small example of the brilliance of this play.

This play has some very funny surprises, so I encourage you to not do too much research, as you do not want these spoilers. Just go to the show with no knowledge of the plot, and you will have a good time.

Regarding Mary's Husband, Julian was fantastic, and had it not been for the insert, I would not have known that Julian does not play this role every show. What was shocking to learn was that this night was actually Julian's debut performing the role. I would happily see Julian in this role again. Julian's performance was excellent alongside Cole's Tony Award-winning performance.

Bianca Leigh and the rest of the cast were also excellent, all contributing to the quality of this show and the resulting experience.

The cast rotates regularly. I am jealous of the folks who have gotten to go back and see every single Mary.

## Art

Performance attended: Wednesday, October 8, 2025 at The Music Box

*Art* by Yasmina Reza is a revival play back on Broadway at The Music Box and directed by Scott Ellis. This production featured major stars Bobby Cannavale, James Corden, and Neil Patrick Harris.

For me, I quickly scheduled this show in order to see Neil Patrick Harris, as I was so upset I missed him in his last show, *Shit. Meet. Fan.* at MCC Theater in 2024.

While all three actors were just outstanding in this play, it was the performance of the character Yvan that is likely going to get James Corden a Tony Award nomination. This Wednesday matinee was the first performance back since Sunday for James, as he had a scheduled absence for the Tuesday show. I was close enough to see in James's eyes that he appeared to be exhausted after his weekend break, and yet he still came out and delivered a show-stopping monologue that finally woke up our sleepy audience.

Audience energy and cast energy can feed off of each other, and this audience was initially worrisome. This was my 55th show of the year yet maybe only the second or third time I had to start the applause, and I was sometimes the only one laughing. I bring this up, because this is where it is a treat to have someone with the skill level of Neil Patrick Harris. His character, Serge, was explaining how his all-white painting actually had other colors in it, and for some reason, I was the only patron who laughed when Serge pointed out it even had red in it. Neil, without missing a beat, broke the fourth wall and had his character give me a stern glare for laughing at the thought there was red in the painting. This finally got the audience to laugh and wake up a bit, and this was all due to Serge very briefly breaking the fourth wall and using nothing more than a facial expression. Genius. I imagine he may do this at every performance, and this was the warm-up that primed the audience for James's intense monologue, which finally got the audience to get into the show. From that moment on, the audience was engaged, and the energy was fantastic.

*Art* is a comedy about the complexity of friendship. While the story is not terribly deep, it was a very good time experiencing three incredible actors doing their magic live on stage. It was very funny.

## Good Night, and Good Luck

Performance attended: Sunday, June 8, 2025 at Winter Garden Theatre

*Good Night, and Good Luck* is based on the true story of Senator Joseph McCarthy and his alleged attacks on journalism and on free speech. The story is specifically about a brave TV reporter who takes on Senator McCarthy, only to have CBS then allegedly targeted by the United States government.

*Good Night, and Good Luck* had its Closing Performance at the Sunday matinee on the same day as the Tony Awards. I am generally not a fan of seeing a show on the same day I am attending the Tony Awards, as the latter is already such a long day, but this was the only free slot in my schedule. And I did want to see this important show before it closed.

I would later learn that the show would do a live broadcast on CNN during the prior performance on Saturday night, Tony Awards Eve. I recorded this performance and am looking forward to watching it again one day. I love this decision to broadcast the show to make it more accessible, as the ticket prices for this show were prohibitively high for many patrons. While seeing a performance on TV is not the same as seeing it live, it is better than not seeing it at all, and viewers still get the excitement of a live show, whereas other televised performances like *Hamilton* on Disney+ are indeed edited after being filmed over multiple performances.

My first observation in this show was just how complex the set was. It almost felt like I was on a movie set, and indeed, I was in a TV news studio. The set felt chaotic at times, especially when action was happening in multiple places at the same time, and I was not always sure where to look. A patron near me exclaimed out loud, "This is crazy!" My interpretation was that this was exactly the point. The newsroom was indeed chaotic during this perilous time in the country. While unsettling at times, which was again likely the point, it worked. The show's chaos stressed me out at times, which reflected the state of society and a newsroom targeted by the government. This set was a unique experience compared to other plays.

I enjoyed the set's incorporation of many old school black and white televisions to show what viewers at home would have been seeing at the time. I tend to think of projections as a modern addition to live theatre, and this was such a creative deployment of modern technology disguised as an old school technology.

## OFF-BROADWAY MUSICALS

### Bat Boy: The Musical

Performance attended: Saturday, November 1, 2025 at New York City Center

"Hold me, Bat Boy!" That's the song I can never get out of my head. Every once in a while, I leave a show thinking, "Wow! That is one of the best shows I've seen this year!" And this was in November. When this happens, I have to take a few days to think about it and make sure I'm not experiencing recency bias.

*Bat Boy: The Musical*, directed by Alex Timbers, had it all: good book, fantastic music, incredible costumes and makeup, lighting design that added to the fun, perfect sound, ridiculous cast, good blocking and choreography, and an amazing creative team. The set was minimal, but it worked just fine. I went into this show just expecting a staged concert with a top cast, and instead I got one of the best musicals I had experienced in 2025, despite limited rehearsal time. I also cannot think of any other show in 2025 where grown men were singing the songs while in the restroom line at intermission.

Lyricist and composer Laurence O'Keefe let us know during a talkback after the show that we were the very first audience to experience the show with the latest revisions, as the creative team had been continuing to tweak and improve the show each day. There were a few scenes where the actors were still "on book" (scripts in hand), but the quality and experience of this cast meant that it did not detract from the performances at all.

Conversely, it was quite impressive how the cast was "off book" in the majority of the scenes, given such little rehearsal time. And some of the cast members were currently in other shows; for example, Christopher Sieber was in *Death Becomes Her*, and Kerry Butler was in *Heathers The Musical*. Christopher did say he pre-arranged a temporary absence from *Death Becomes Her* during this short run of *Bat Boy*.

This story and book by Keythe Farley and Brian Flemming is so fun, and the music and lyrics by O'Keefe are just fantastic. It is a fun original cast recording to listen to over and over, although the new production does seem to now differ a bit from the original cast recording. It may be time for a new cast recording!

It was explained to us during the post-show talkback that *Bat Boy* was really wanted for an *Encores!* performance, but New York City Center will only consider shows that have been on Broadway for *Encores!* performances. *Bat Boy* has not been on Broadway YET, was the exact statement, and they therefore chose it to be the annual gala performance instead.

The 2024 gala performance was *Ragtime*, and we now know what happened next with that show. Fingers crossed for *Bat Boy*!

While Bat Boy the character could be a metaphor for anyone who is different and just trying to fit in, it was autism and neurodiversity that was on my mind throughout the show. In the case of an autistic and/or neurodivergent person, the initial tendency can be to try and change the person to be more "normal" and to "fit in." Eventually, you realize that "normal" people can actually learn from the neurodivergent person, and perhaps it is the neurotypical person who actually needs to change and adapt. *Bat Boy: The Musical* makes this point. After the talkback, I asked Laurence O'Keefe if an autism metaphor was intentional, and he said while it was not intentional, the creative team had definitely noticed this, and he said I was not the first patron to ask about this.

Many patrons never notice the lighting design, but in *Bat Boy*, there was some very fun use of lighting, especially in Act I, that gets quite a few laughs (also due to the sound design). The only other time I can recall lighting design getting laughs was when the lighting in *Hamilton* turns blue when King George III sings that he is so blue. The *Bat Boy* lighting design by Justin Townsend was a highlight in this production, especially considering the intentionally simple set. The scenic design by David Korins worked very well.

If this performance were on Broadway, I would expect to see makeup designer Suki Tsujimoto getting a Tony Award nomination specifically for the Bat Boy character. Jennifer Moeller and Rob Pickens similarly did outstanding work with costume design and hair and wig design, respectively.

In addition to the visually stunning effects, Andrew Resnick (music director), Ben Green and Laurence O'Keefe (orchestrations and arrangements), Nevin Steinberg (sound design), and Kimberlee Wertz (music coordinator) made sure our ears were happy. The music and sound were as close to perfect as you can get in this production.

The remainder of this fantastic creative team included puppet and props design by Ray Wetmore and JR Goodman, production stage manager Cynthia Cahill, and choreography by Connor Gallagher.

I came into this show primarily familiar just with Christopher Sieber, Andrew Durand, and Alex Newell, but I was aware of Taylor Trensch's work in *Floyd Collins*, which I sadly missed.

Let's start with Taylor Trensch, as this was one of the best performances I experienced in 2025. Darren Criss received a Tony Award for his work as Oliver in *Maybe Happy Ending*, largely for his physical acting, and I feel like Bat Boy is Oliver on steroids. Oliver and Bat Boy are both characters where we see their behaviors, movements, and communication evolve over the course of the show. Just as Darren did a phenomenal job evolving Oliver over the course of the story, Taylor has done the same here with Bat Boy. One reason I would have loved to see *Bat Boy* again would be just to study Taylor's performance a bit more. If this show can transfer to Broadway and with Taylor still in the role, he surely would be a top contender for the Tony Award for "Best Performance by a Leading Actor in a Musical."

Next, I really loved the performances of Kerry Butler and Gabi Carrubba as mother and daughter. A fun fact is that Kerry played the role of the daughter in its Off-Broadway production in 2001, and now she is playing her mom. While I sometimes felt like I was watching twins on stage, the casting of these two worked so well. They have great chemistry together, they are both fantastic actors and singers, and it was a treat to experience their performances. I am so jealous of the people I have met who saw Kerry as Shelley in the original production. At least I can hear her as Shelley in the original cast recording. Count me in as a new big fan of these two.

When I was scheduling *Death Becomes Her*, I quickly realized from watching clips that I needed to not only prioritize a show with both Jennifer Simard and Megan Hilty, who had a reduced schedule at the time, but I also needed to make sure I picked a show where Christopher Sieber was not on a scheduled absence. His character is a bit underrated in *Death Becomes Her*, and Christopher was so good. I hope to be able to see him again when I go back to see Betsy Wolfe in the show. I came into *Bat Boy* excited to see Christopher again, and he did not disappoint. As he stated during the talkback, he worked hard to NOT try to be funny, as he knew that the more serious he was, the more hilarious his performance would be.

I became a fan of Andrew Durand in *Shucked*. I later saw Andrew perform in *Little Shop of Horrors*, which I will talk about later in this book. Andrew was fantastic in *Bat Boy*, as expected.

*Shucked* is also where I discovered Alex Newell, and they seem to have even more command of the stage in *Bat Boy*. Alex was clearly a fan favorite, and their appearance in *Bat Boy* felt similar to when Michelle Williams appeared in *Death Becomes Her*. The crowd goes wild, and then we experienced the treat of an excellent performance.

I knew I had seen Alan H. Green before, but I couldn't place him. Now I know! I saw him in the pre-Broadway run of *The Griswolds' Broadway Vacation* in 2022 at The 5th Avenue Theatre in Seattle, where he was hilarious. Jacob Ming-Trent as Reverend Hightown also gave us a very fun and entertaining performance in *Bat Boy*.

The entire cast was outstanding, and the consistent quality across the board was part of what made this show so good. The rest of this fantastic cast included Mary Faber, Evan Harrington, John-Michael Lyles, Tom McGowan, Olivia Puckett, Marissa Rosen, Colin Trudell, Rema Webb, and Marissa Jaret Winokur. Understudies were August Bagg, Will Mann, and Stephanie Reuning-Scherer.

I always advise tourists to prioritize shows with the original cast and/or shows closing soon. Due to this short run and this phenomenal cast, this was obviously a show to prioritize high on the list of must-see shows. But hopefully, there will be chances to see this fun show again and on Broadway.

## Mexodus

Performances attended: Monday, October 6 and Saturday, November 1, 2025 at Audible's Minetta Lane Theatre

*Disclosure: I am a co-producer of this show. That's how much I liked it.*

*Mexodus* was a show I prioritized seeing after hearing so much buzz about it. I knew exactly where I wanted to sit, since I had seen *Sexual Misconduct of the Middle Classes* at this same venue, Audible's Minetta Lane Theatre, back in June.

A primary "wow" factor with *Mexodus* was the live-looping on stage, but the show also has a great story, teaches us some history we did not know (bonus!), and the music is as beautiful as is the story.

How do you present a story about survival, xenophobia, racism, slavery, friendship, and hope and make it fresh and fun? Brian Quijada and Nygel D. Robinson figured out they could do so with a live-looped musical, where they created the show's beautiful music live on stage each night. The music is fantastic, the lyrics are deep, and the acting and emotional performances provided the exclamation point. You both laugh and cry, and the experience was just incredible.

To get a sample of the show's music, head over to your favorite music streaming service, and search for *Mexodus*. You should then be presented with the song, "Two Bodies (from *Mexodus*)" as a part of your search results.

The first patron comments I overheard at the end of the show were, "I want to see that again!" (I agree).

Both Brian and Nygel were brilliant performers and a joy to watch on stage.

In this production, I especially enjoyed the costumes, the sound design, the scenic design, and I also enjoyed the choreography and stage movement throughout the 90 minutes. The music is fun to listen to again and again.

Scenic design was by Riw Rakkulchon, costume design was by director David Mendizábal, lighting design was by Mextly Couzin, looping systems architecture and sound design was by Mikhail Fiksel, projection design was by Johnny Moreno, and orchestrations were by Mikhail Fiksel, Brian Quijada, and Nygel D. Robinson. Choreography was by Tony Thomas. Hope Villanueva was production stage manager.

## JOY: A New True Musical

Performance attended: Monday, July 14, 2025 at Laura Pels Theatre at the Harold and Miriam Steinberg Center for Theatre

The main reason I went to see *JOY* was because Betsy Wolfe was in the cast. I became a fan of hers when I saw her in *& Juliet* in 2023, and I plan to hopefully see her again when I go back to see *Death Becomes Her* again.

Parenting is hard, especially for a working single parent. Add in sexism, financial stress, and unsupportive loved ones, and it can be hard to find the strength to keep pushing forward. Enter Joy Mangano, single mom and inventor of the Miracle Mop. This is her story.

When I got the e-mail inviting me to an upcoming Off-Broadway show called *JOY: A New True Musical*, I was sold pretty quickly as soon as I saw the name Betsy Wolfe. Betsy had been who I was cheering for at the 76th Annual Tony Awards in 2023 for her role as Anne Hathaway (no, not that Anne Hathaway) in *& Juliet*. Betsy has also been Jenna in *Waitress*, one of my all-time favorite musicals. In other words, Betsy has credibility in the roles she picks.

As mentioned, *JOY* is the story of Joy Mangano, who invented the Miracle Mop. There is a related movie starring Jennifer Lawrence, Robert De Niro, and Bradley Cooper.

*JOY* has a good balance of comedy and tackling emotional issues. But *JOY* also reminds me why I love musicals, because a musical can insert a hilarious musical number that you just do not get in a play. The first QVC musical number in Act 1 of *JOY* was so funny.

I came into this show with very high expectations of Betsy Wolfe, because I loved her performance in *& Juliet* so much. Betsy handled my high expectations just fine, and her vocals and acting were outstanding. She was also lovely out of character when meeting her after the show.

I was also very impressed with Honor Blue Savage's performance, especially considering her age. She played Joy's daughter, Christie, and she had acting skills I sometimes do not see in adult actors. I observed she was always acting, even when in the background, and her facial expressions and energy level stood out.

Paul Whitty, as Cowboy Eddie, was also a standout for me, and I felt like this was really good casting for this part. His performance was fun, and I can imagine it would be such a good time to play this "bad guy" character.

The rest of the cast was solid, and the cowboy musical number in Act 2 was a close second place to the QVC musical number in Act 1. These fun musical numbers were a nice supplement to the beautiful solos, especially the ones by Betsy.

I am picky about sound engineering, so I want to give a shout out to Jacob for doing a perfect job at the show I attended. It is so rare to have perfect sound engineering, and quality sound engineering is one of my favorite reasons to see a show in New York.

Betsy's incredible vocals combined with perfect sound engineering made my ears and brain very happy.

## OFF-BROADWAY PLAYS

### Caroline

Performance attended: Sunday, October 5, 2025 at MCC Theater

*Caroline* by Preston Max Allen is one of the best plays I have ever experienced. Full stop. It was directed by David Cromer, who recently directed the Broadway productions of *Dead Outlaw* and *Good Night, and Good Luck.*

*Caroline* is the beautiful story about the relationship between a struggling single mom and her nine-year-old transgender daughter. When the mother, Maddie, needs to take her daughter, Caroline, out of town due to transphobic violence, she takes her daughter to her parents' house. This is the first time Maddie's parents learn they have a nine-year-old granddaughter and the first time they have seen Maddie in many years. The relationship between Maddie and her parents is complicated and full of history related to substance abuse, class issues, and more.

The story feels very realistic and is so timely. The audience is offered a good balance of laughing and crying throughout the play.

Chloë Grace Moretz's performance as Maddie, a mother and a daughter, was just outstanding, and she taught us what good motherhood actually looks like. I very much enjoyed her performance, and I want to tell Maddie I am so proud of her. I can't wait to see Chloë on stage again in the future.

Amy Landecker as Rhea, the mother and grandmother, similarly delivered an excellent performance, and I found myself still upset with her long after the play was over. Only very good writing and acting can make you feel the feels hours after the show is over.

And last but not least, River Lipe-Smith was fantastic as Caroline. My favorite moment in her acting was when she completely changed her mood early in the show after her mother used her new name for the first time.

All three performers in this cast were just so excellent in conveying their emotions throughout the story.

I also really enjoyed the set (scenic design by Lee Jellinek), and the patron sitting next to me and I had a full discussion about the set before the show even started. We noticed little details like the thermostat on the wall, and later, I really enjoyed something as simple as the light in the built-in refrigerator. There was really good attention to detail with this set.

The costume design by David Hyman was also very good, and in particular, I understood Rhea's character before she even spoke, partly due to her clothing (and partly due to her posture). The same was true of Maddie's costumes.

The sound design by Christopher Darbassie also had very minor details that I noticed and that made a positive contribution to the experience. The lighting design by Tyler Micoleau was also very good.

This talented creative team also included Robert Pickens (hair and wig design), Suki Tsujimoto (makeup design), Gigi Buffington (voice and text coach), Samantha Shoffner (props supervisor), and Nicole Johnson, Em Chester / Harriet Tubman Effect as DEI consultant. Casting is by The Telsey Office / Caparelliotis Casting.

I have been advocating to local theatres to program this show, as this show needs to live on. It is so good.

## Sexual Misconduct of the Middle Classes

Performance attended: Tuesday, June 10, 2025 at Audible's Minetta Lane Theatre

*Sexual Misconduct of the Middle Classes* is about an inappropriate relationship between a college professor and a student, but what if that professor is likable and what if the college student is the one coming on to the professor? Don't worry, the playwright knows what she is doing. The casting of a likable male lead, where the audience might have empathy, just helps the playwright put an exclamation point on making her point in the end. The casting of this play was excellent, and the story is fantastic.

I have always regretted not seeing Hugh Jackman and Sutton Foster in *The Music Man* when I was in New York in 2022, and the show closed prior to my next trip in 2023. And after seeing *Purpose* in July, I learned about *Appropriate* by the same playwright, and I similarly regret not seeing Ella Beatty in *Appropriate* in 2024. This regret has created urgency for me to see original casts with performers I love before the show closes. Case in point: *Redwood*. I did my job and had my ticket, but it was sadly canceled and refunded before I got into town. Other examples are *The Jonathan Larson Project* (missed it), *SMASH* (got in before it closed!), *Sondheim's Old Friends* (got in before it closed!), and a little Off-Broadway play called *Sexual Misconduct of the Middle Classes*.

For my first trip of 2025, I had done my research and discovered that Hugh was performing in this Off-Broadway play at Minetta Lane Theatre. The only catch was that I would have to extend my trip to see the play, as it was not playing at all during my dates I had booked in NYC.

I booked a front row seat for the play at its first show back on Tuesday, June 10, and I decided to go ahead and extend my stay until that Friday. Thanks to this show's schedule, I was able to also add in *Oh, Mary!*, *Maybe Happy Ending*, *Sunset Blvd.*, and *Just In Time*. In other words, Hugh gets credit for me getting to see some of the best shows I have ever seen! Thanks, Hugh!

Prior to the show starting, a woman came on stage and started rearranging the furniture and set pieces in this play's minimal setup. At the time, you might assume it was tech crew running a bit behind on their duties, as they usually perform these tasks before the house opens. But sometimes things go wrong right before the show. I eventually realized this stagehand was actually Ella Beatty! I absolutely love it when directors start the show before the show's curtain time. This preshow detail ended up being significant to the story.

The woman sitting next to me was barely awake, and she eventually explained she is an ICU nurse from London, and she flew into NYC for one night only, just to see Hugh Jackman. She was able to meet Hugh and get a picture with him before the show. At one point in the show, Hugh sat down at the edge of the stage, and he was immediately in front of us. I glanced at her, and she was clearly in heaven. Her one night travel adventure was worth it!

Early in the show, Hugh began pushing a cordless lawnmower across the wooden stage floor. It was a brilliant prop, as I cannot think of a more efficient way for the playwright to let us know the character is outdoors on his lawn, presumably in front of his house. So efficient, and the character didn't need to announce to us that he was in his yard. We firmly believed that wooden stage floor was absolutely a lawn. Hugh knew how to deliver it just perfectly, so it was also just the right amount of funny that a somewhat noisy lawnmower was in use on stage.

If you had read about this performance, you would know that Hugh sometimes interacted with the audience. At our show, he said "bless you" to a patron who sneezed, and later, when an audience member sneezed so violently that we all jumped in our chairs, he of course addressed it, causing quite a bit of laughter in the audience, before he finally went back to, "now where was I?"

As the title suggests, the play covers a very serious subject matter, and Hugh indeed made us cringe multiple times throughout the show. The story works perfectly with a male lead where you might want to have just a bit of empathy (we love Hugh, right?). And then the playwright uses this empathy against you and reminds you that people who do bad things can be charismatic.

At the end of the show, you understand why the show started the way it did. I left this trip feeling like I had seen one of the best plays I had ever seen (yes, this was a theme in 2025 where I saw some of the best plays of my life). I was excited to later learn that the very first reading of this play was actually at my hometown theatre, Seattle Rep, years earlier.

While Ella and Hugh were fantastic casting, this story by Hannah Moscovitch can stand on its own and be excellent with any talented cast. I do always enjoy discovering new talent, and it was a pleasure to discover Ella Beatty's talent (and I wish I had seen her in *Appropriate* in 2024!).

## KYOTO

Performance attended: Thursday, October 9, 2025 at Lincoln Center Theater at the Mitzi E. Newhouse

After success in London's West End, *KYOTO* arrived in New York with much of the cast coming over from London.

This was my seventh show of the week and my 57th show of the year, so I was not thrilled to learn the runtime was 2 hours and 45 minutes. My happy place is when the usher tells me, "90 minutes, no intermission." But there is nothing I would cut from this show, and the show would actually be much longer if it were not for the exceptional pacing. I do not know if I have ever before complimented the pacing of a preview performance, as pacing is most often the issue in a preview, but wow, the pacing in this show was just terrific. The almost three hours flew by, and I was on the edge of my seat from the moment the show started until the end. It was advertised as a thriller, and indeed this show was very thrilling and entertaining.

The show was also immersive if you choose one of the conference table seats at the edge of the stage. They assure you that you will not be expected to participate, but there was quite a bit of interaction with the cast. I had an actor sitting immediately next to me for most of the show, and another actor was two seats away. They addressed me quite often, but it was up to me whether or not I wanted to respond. We also all got to wear lanyards indicating whether we were delegates or media. It was all very fun.

From the start, the production reminded me of elements of *Just In Time*, even though the stories are very different. Just as Jonathan Groff welcomes you to *Wicked*'s basement, he could have similarly come over here and said, "Welcome to the show in *Ragtime*'s basement." The two basement venues are similar in that they are both in the round, they are both small and intimate, both shows are immersive, and both are directly beneath a show with a lot of buzz. While *Ragtime* may have had all of the buzz at Lincoln Center Theater, *KYOTO* holds its own as an outstanding production and patron experience. And this was only its second performance in New York. Wow!

*KYOTO* is based on a true story where the world actually does come together in the late 1990s for climate change action. The cast was fantastic, and this was a very high quality production. *KYOTO* is one of my favorite plays of 2025.

The play is written by Joe Murphy and Joe Robertson and was directed by Stephen Daldry and Justin Martin. The company is large, and the full cast list and creative team are listed on Lincoln Center Theater's website.

Stephen Kunken's performance as real-life Republican oil lobbyist Don Pearlman was exceptional.

This show truly is a thriller, and it was non-stop entertainment. Making the production immersive and intimate just added to the experience of an already excellent story.

## Twelfth Night

Performance attended: Friday, September 5, 2025 at The Public's Delacorte Theater in Central Park

*Twelfth Night, or What You Will* was my first time experiencing Free Shakespeare in the Park. This was the first show back at The Delacorte Theater, in the middle of Central Park, after the venue received a major renovation. The venue is truly beautiful. The staff members were also very friendly.

With *Twelfth Night*, like with many Shakespeare plays, there is a balancing act between how long you make the play and how deep you go with the story. This play could likely be anywhere between 90 minutes and five hours long. The last production I saw earlier in 2025 was a tad under three hours long, which just felt a bit on the long side (but was still very good and enjoyable). I see so many shows that I am always thrilled when a show is under two hours and without an intermission. This production was 1 hour 55 minutes long with no intermission, which is a nice sweet spot. Some critics wished it were longer with more depth, but I argue this length was just right, as this show is fine as a comedy.

I knew going in that this was a standout cast, so the surprises for me were the set, the costumes, and the special effects. The set revealed itself as far more complex than you would expect as the show progressed, and this was such a pleasant surprise given it was an outdoor venue. The costumes were absolutely stunning. And the special effects were similarly surprising given the venue. This production exceeded my expectations in so many areas.

Jesse Tyler Ferguson had been on my bucket list for a while to see perform (check!), and he was very funny and entertaining as Andrew Aguecheek. I love Peter Dinklage as a TV and movie star, but those skills do not always transfer to live stage, so I was cautious with my expectations of Peter. Peter was so excellent on stage that I quickly realized he was not new to stage; I confirmed he indeed was an experienced stage actor, not just a film actor, and it showed in his performance. Like Jesse, Peter was especially skilled in his physical acting, too. This entire cast was so loaded with talent that I am not going to mention everyone; the cast was balanced, and each performer was excellent. It is such a treat when there is not a standout performer, due to the entire cast being so good.

I will call out director Saheem Ali for such great choices throughout the show. I especially enjoyed how much music was in the production. This may have been my first Shakespeare in the Park, but it will not be my last. I will attempt to make this an annual occurrence now.

## SEATTLE MUSICALS

### Come From Away

Performances attended: Wednesday, November 26, Wednesday, December 3, and Saturday, January 3, 2026 at Seattle Rep

Without a doubt, the 10-year anniversary production of *Come From Away* was one of the greatest shows in 2025. I attended Invited Dress, Opening Night, Closing Weekend, and a benefit concert called *Cut From Away*, where (really good!) songs that were cut from the musical were performed. It was like getting to see an extended version of the musical.

Based on a true story, *Come From Away* is the feel-good,

must-see musical about diverse humans coming together after the terrorist attacks in the United States on September 11, 2001. This updated 10th Anniversary production was as timely as ever. Book, music, and lyrics are by Irene Sankoff and David Hein.

Because there are at least five different years and two different 10th anniversaries involved, allow me to first explain the math, since you may be confused if you know this show was on Broadway in 2017 (not ten years ago). Prior to the successful Broadway run in 2017, *Come From Away* first had success in 2015 as a co-production between Seattle Rep and La Jolla Playhouse. This new production directed by Brandon Ivie was the 10th anniversary of the 2015 start at Seattle Rep.

Furthermore, the story also involves a different 10th anniversary when the "come from aways" return 10 years later for a reunion on September 11, 2011. Ivie cleverly incorporated the story's 10th anniversary into this production's 10th anniversary by having this production's story start in 2011, not 2001. Those familiar with the original production may recall the story ends with this reunion, as it does here, too, but we now also start with the reunion in order to make the experience more immersive.

I'm a big fan of shows that actually start prior to the curtain time, and this production started the moment your ticket was scanned. I always tell people to get to their seats early, as you never know when a director will make this choice to start the show before the show. Other examples that come to mind where the show starts early, while the house lights are still up, include *MJ the Musical*, *Maybe Happy Ending*, and of course *The Play That Goes Wrong*. I love this choice whenever a director chooses to set the mood well before curtain time.

In this case, as soon as your ticket was scanned, you entered the 10 year reunion festivities on September 11, 2011. There was a handout that directed you to various activities, and you could even go on stage to get a drink, since you were now one of the "come from aways" just like the other characters. If you paid close attention, you would have noticed that various characters were arriving on stage and greeting each other after not having seen each other for ten years. Again, this was all prior to the official start and while the house lights were still on.

This set was very nicely done. I had previously noticed with *Liberation* on Broadway just how much detail goes into creating a gymnasium, and this set does it just as well. Tim Mackabee was the Scenic Designer for this production.

Perhaps what jumped out at me more than anything in this production was the lighting design by Robert J. Aguilar. I regularly tell people that lighting design is one of the biggest differences between shows in New York and Seattle. The lighting in this production of *Come From Away* was just stunning. When you combined this intimate venue size (similar to a small Broadway house), this set, and this lighting design, it indeed felt like you were in a Broadway house seeing a Broadway production. I have seen more shows in New York than in Seattle this year, and this production's lighting design beats out many of the shows I have seen in New York this year. Lighting can be so powerful, and Aguilar has done an incredible job.

It was so impressive to see the talent on this stage. Do we call this a quadruple threat? This cast of actor-musicians not only brought the acting, singing, and dancing, but they brought their talents with musical instruments as well. My daughter pointed out to me how the hilarious cardiologist scene was even better with the addition of the guitars. Am I the only one who wishes that scene was just a few seconds longer? So fun. Chris Ranney was Music Supervisor and Conductor, Elisa Money was Associate Music Director, and Ken Travis was Sound Designer. This was a show where you may find yourself listening to the Original Broadway Cast Recording over and over again, as this music is just so good.

Costume Designer An-lin Dauber had an important job in this show, as there were just so many characters! Actors played numerous characters each, and the costumes helped us keep track of who was who. In this story, you really should not be noticing the costumes if done well, and the costumes did their job perfectly. This show did a really nice job with quick changes—often happening right on stage—and the costumes were effective. I was never once confused, despite so many characters, and it was impressive how these actors shifted from character to character—and from costume to costume—so frequently.

Another area where this production excelled was with Kate Myre's dialect coaching. And last but not least on the creative front, choreographer William Carlos Angulo and Dance Captain Cedric Lamar, along with Ivie, did a very nice job with all of the stage movement. There was nice coordination between this movement and the lighting and sound, which of course speaks just as loudly as the script.

There were too many cast members to mention them all, and what I really appreciated was the balance of this cast and how they were each excellent. I sometimes view it as a negative if one or two actors stand out significantly more than the rest of the cast, and I like how each actor was excellent in this production—and for multiple characters each! My daughter commented she was surprised how much this cast looked like the original cast, and then she couldn't believe it when I added that some of them also appeared very similar to the real life humans these characters are based on. The casting was excellent even when you do not consider they are also actor-musicians.

I started to write about my favorite actors, favorite storylines, and favorite characters, but then I realized they were actually all my favorites.

If you are not familiar with the story, you might be

concerned this subject matter is too heavy. Rest assured you will smile and laugh a lot (yes you will also cry), and this is a feel-good, heartwarming story despite the heavy moments.

## After Midnight

Performance attended: Friday, August 8, 2025 at The 5th Avenue Theatre (Seattle)

*After Midnight* is a jazz musical revue full of live jazz on stage, vocals, and dancing, taking place "after midnight" in Harlem at the Cotton Club. The show features Duke Ellington's music and the Jazz Age of the Harlem Renaissance. The Broadway production of the same name was based on an earlier revue called *Cotton Club Parade*.

*After Midnight* was one of the highest quality productions I have experienced at The 5th Avenue Theatre Company in Seattle.

While *After Midnight* is primarily known for its music and choreography (more on this in a bit), it was the lighting that made the first impression on me. And this was before the show even started. What I learned again was that a production that just has a curtain closed until the show starts, as so many shows do, misses out on an opportunity to set the mood and the atmosphere from the moment the audience walks in. For me, when I first walked in, the combination of the visible set and the lighting had an immediate impact on me. I regularly tell people that one big difference between shows in New York and shows in Seattle is the lighting, as the lighting is just so often stunning in New York shows. This was a very good lighting design, so kudos to lighting designer Xavier Pierce.

I started asking patrons sitting near me, "Is it my imagination, or is the house lighting a bit dimmer than usual, perhaps in order to create a mood? Or is this feeling I am having simply due to the stage lighting?" These patrons mostly did not validate my reaction to the lighting, so I decided I needed to ask someone more in the know. The unanswered question was starting to bug me. I really wanted to know if they intentionally dimmed the house lighting, as I thought it would be so creative if they did so. I finally walked over to director Jay Santos, who was conveniently just a few feet away from me (it was Opening Night), and I asked her my question. She was gracious and explained to me that while the house lights were set the same as they always are, she validated my reaction and told me it was indeed intentional to create this atmosphere prior to the show starting. It was very fun to see how much impact (at least for me) pre-show decisions like the lighting design can have before the show even starts. A simple closed curtain just seems like such a lost opportunity. The lighting was consistently stunning throughout the show.

As for the choreography, in the 2013 Broadway production, *After Midnight* won the 2014 Tony Award for "Best Choreography." It also won the Drama Desk Awards for "Outstanding Musical Revue" and "Outstanding Choreography," as well as the Outer Critics Circle Award for "Outstanding Choreographer." Pamela Yasutake was the choreographer for The 5th Avenue Theatre Company's production, and the dancing and stage movement in this production did not disappoint. The year 2025 had so far been an excellent year for outstanding choreography in shows on Broadway, and this Seattle production was again just like being at a New York show.

William Knowles was the Music Director, and the music and the musicians in this show were of course major highlights. What I enjoyed most about this orchestra was actually not their incredible music but rather seeing the musicians smile so much in between songs. They perhaps did not mean to smile so much but just could not help it. They were truly having so much fun, and their smiles made me smile. It just felt like they were having one of the best nights of their lives, and their joy added to my joy.

Director Jay Santos and this entire creative team somehow managed to turn the large 5th Avenue Theatre into an intimate, immersive experience. There were cabaret tables where the orchestra pit usually is located (the band was on stage), and the cast periodically came down the steps to perform within the orchestra seating section. This experience reminded me at times of *Just In Time* on Broadway, where the Circle in the Square Theatre has been converted into a nightclub.

When you have an incredible lighting design, you had better have incredible costumes, and costume designer Ricky German came through. There were a few standout costumes, and all of them added to the quality of the experience.

One of my pet peeves, especially if there is singing, is poor sound engineering, and The 5th Avenue Theatre consistently does a good job in this department. Sound designer Justin Stasiw and all of the sound engineers involved in this production did a flawless job on Opening Night.

I enjoyed the performances of each of the cast members equally, as the cast was balanced with flawless performances across the board. This top talent cast included Iris Beaumier, Nicholas Japaul Bernard, Brian Davis, Nalica Hennings, Jason Holley, Nehemiah Hooks, Trina Mills, Yusef Seevers, Porscha Shaw, and Madison Willis. Understudies included Savannah Cooper, Alysha Morgan, Stanley Martin, and Lamont Brown. Trina Mills was the dance captain.

The orchestra included William Knowles, Rebecca Smith, Chris Patin, Lamar Lofton, Brian Bermudez, Jovon Miller, Alex Dugdale, Owuor Arunga, Nathan Breedlove, Beserat Tafesse, and Kimberly Rosenberg.

## SEATTLE PLAYS

## Fancy Dancer

Performances attended: Wednesday, September 24 and Sunday, October 26, 2025 at Seattle Rep with Seattle Children's Theatre

There is a very fun play called *The Thanksgiving Play*, written by Larissa FastHorse. But before Larissa was an award-winning playwright, she was a dancer. *Fancy Dancer* is her story.

*Fancy Dancer* is a special play. It is one of my all-time favorite plays. I feel grateful for getting to experience it on Opening Night of its World Premiere, and I went back to see it again.

If you have ever been told you can't do that, you aren't good enough, or you are too different, you will be inspired by this story.

The playwright Larissa FastHorse was in Seattle from her home in Los Angeles to perform this one-person show on specific dates, and she is as skilled as an actor as she is as a playwright. If you recognize her name, it is likely because of the hilarious and witty *The Thanksgiving Play*, which I had the joy of experiencing in October 2023 at Tacoma Arts Live. *The Thanksgiving Play* made its Broadway debut in 2023 and was nominated for multiple Drama League Awards and won a Theatre World Award.

She also wrote the recent *Peter Pan: The Broadway Musical* but without the harmful stereotypes. I recall being a bit nervous taking my kids to see a Peter Pan story in 2024, as I remembered the harmful parts of the story, and I was so pleasantly surprised with the revisions.

Select performances of *Fancy Dancer*, produced by Seattle Rep and Seattle Children's Theatre, were performed by actor-dancer Burgandi Trejo Phoenix.

In addition to the stellar acting and powerful script, director Chay Yew exceeded my expectations with the production quality. I see so many shows that I have developed a pet peeve for a show that doesn't take the opportunity to set the mood before the show even starts. A closed curtain with no other thought just feels like a missed opportunity. *Fancy Dancer* used a combination of projections and sound design to create a thunderstorm with gentle rain to greet you as you found your seat. While I do not always like how projections are implemented, I actually really enjoyed the extensive use of projections throughout this show, and the sound design was similarly thoughtful. These details contributed to my positive experience.

The scenic design was by Junghyun Georgia Lee, lighting design was by Geoff Korf, sound design was by Robertson Witmer, costumes were by Mary Kelsay, and choreography was by Price Suddarth and Maxine Alex. Jayna Shoda Meyer was Associate Director, Caite Hevner and Ann Slote were responsible for the projections, Gin Hammond was Local Vocal Consultant, and Cristine Reynolds was the Stage Manager.

## The Play That Goes Wrong

Performances attended: Tuesday, August 27 and Tuesday, September 23, 2025 at Seattle Rep (and Thursday, July 17, 2025 at New World Stages)

*The Play That Goes Wrong* is part of a series of "Goes Wrong" productions developed by the British theatre company Mischief Theatre. The fictional Cornley Polytechnic Drama Society features fictional actors that star in all of the shows, so there is always a show within the show that features a cast within the cast. The detail and complexity of the humor (humour?) are just as entertaining as the shows themselves.

This local production, a joint production of Seattle Rep and

Portland Center Stage, got in on the fun with a Know Before You Go e-mail that messed up your show date by many months and "lost dog" flyers placed throughout the Seattle Rep venue. Poor Winston. In New York, I was one of the patrons who was approached by crew members asking if I had seen a dog running around.

I first learned about this series many years ago when I discovered the TV show, *A Christmas Carol Goes Wrong*. I typically watch this show at least once per holiday season. I have no idea how many times I have watched it. You can usually find it on BroadwayHD or Amazon Prime, depending on current licensing arrangements.

*Peter Pan Goes Wrong*, which actually debuted on TV before *A Christmas Carol Goes Wrong*, is similarly hilarious, and it actually had a Broadway debut in 2023 after previously only having been on stage in the UK. I had the joy of meeting two of the three creators and playwrights, Henry Lewis and Jonathan Sayer, when they were in New York City for a run of *Peter Pan Goes Wrong*. They were both so kind and fun to chat with.

Another one of their popular television productions is *The Goes Wrong Show* series, which is the most similar to this play. What I especially enjoyed was how the fictional actors were so similar with their unique personality quirks from show to show. In newer productions without the original cast, like the current Off-Broadway production and this current Seattle production, you can find these consistent quirks in some of the cast members but not all. Some of the actors have worked to mimic the behaviors of the original cast members, while other actors have decided to make the characters their own. For long-term fans like me, I really appreciate it when I immediately know who the fictional actor character is even when the physical appearance is very different. For patrons not familiar with the show, it of course will not matter. Just know that if you now go watch the TV shows or the other stage productions, you will see this consistency in the fictional actors from show to show, which I find to be very fun.

This is an important show to get to your seat early, both before Act I and again during intermission. And then pay attention. Everything that appears chaotic, before the house lights are even turned down, is of course scripted and part of the show.

British humour is not for everyone, and you can watch one of the TV shows mentioned previously to find out if this is your cup of tea. I find the writing in this series of shows to be brilliant, and you probably need to see the show multiple times in order to catch all that is going on.

In this local production, the cast was fantastic. This show is a lot of fun and one you want to see again and again.

## An Enemy of the People

Performance attended: Sunday, September 28, 2025 at ACT Theatre at Union Arts Center

Before we had Jonathan Groff performing in Circle in the Square Theatre in 2025, we had an updated adaptation of Henrik Ibsen's 1882 play, *An Enemy of the People*, in this intimate Broadway venue in 2024. This adaptation of *An Enemy of the People* on Broadway was created by the award-winning playwright Amy Herzog, who won the 2024 Drama Desk Award for "Outstanding Adaptation" for this play. The play also received a 2024 Tony Award nomination for "Best Revival of a Play" in the same year she also received a Tony Award nomination for "Best Play" with *Mary Jane*. In other words, this adaptation of *An Enemy of the People* is fresh, vetted on Broadway, and very good. What better venue to bring this award-winning play to than the similar Allen Theatre at Union Arts Center, where we are also treated to the intimacy of theatre in the round?

Director Victor Pappas has taken this incredible work of

Amy Herzog, based on the classic by Henrik Ibsen, assembled a top notch cast and creative team, and put together a high quality production that was both entertaining and meaningful.

"That was timely" was the comment from the patron behind me when the lights went down at the end of the show. While it may feel disheartening that a story written in 1882 that we should have learned from is once again relevant, this recurring issue with humans is actually acknowledged in the story. The story highlights the complexities and differing perspectives of challenging situations when not everyone has the same values, ethics, or motives.

The cast was excellent. The set, costumes, lighting, and sound were also top notch. The choreography, especially at the end of the show, was incredible.

The cast included Bjorn Anders, Tommy Beale, Shawn Belyea, Aaron Blakely, Bradford Farwell, Daniel Hanlon, Lee Ann Hittenberger, Nehemiah Hooks, Josh Kenji Langager, Alanah Pascual, Robert Shampain, Ricky Spaulding, and Jace Tucker.

The creative team included Matthew Smucker (scenic design), Cathy Hunt (costume design), Connie Yun (lighting design), Thorn Michaels (assistant lighting design), Dominic CodyKramers (sound design), Robertson Witmer (composer), Alyssa Keene (dialect coach), Geoffrey Alm (fight director), Rachel Nesvig (hardanger fiddle and violin), and Grant Olson (cello). Melissa Y. Hamasaki was stage manager, and Nicola Krause was assistant stage manager.

*An Enemy of the People* was the first show of the 2025-26 season, which was the first season with ACT and Seattle Shakespeare merged under the new name Union Arts Center.

## Dial M for Murder

Performance attended: Friday, January 24, 2025 at Village Theatre (Issaquah, Washington)

My second show of 2025 was *Dial M for Murder* at Village Theatre in Issaquah, Washington. It was Opening Night, and I was attending to support the local superstar Angela DiMarco. Angela has a gift in that she is an incredible stage actor as well as a phenomenal film actor, and she actually teaches classes to help actors better understand and learn the differences between stage acting and film acting. I have had the pleasure of seeing her perform both on the big screen as well as on stage, and she is one of my favorite actors. She was outstanding in this excellent production—the best show I have seen at Village Theatre in quite a while—and this show was well worth the drive from Bainbridge Island to Issaquah.

It was also a nice surprise to see R. Hamilton Wright show up on stage (I had not yet looked at the cast list), as I also always enjoy his performances. He is also active behind the scenes supporting local theatre, which is always appreciated.

Keep an eye on Angela, as she has some exciting film projects underway as of 2026.

# 3

# LOBBY TALK

This next section includes the shows I loved in 2025 but where I have less to say. This is not due to loving these shows any less but rather due to having fewer notes on these shows, primarily due to time constraints.

There are indeed shows in this section, for example *Beau the Musical* and *The Bridges of Madison County* Original Broadway Cast Reunion Concert, that I absolutely loved even more than some of the shows I wrote more about in the prior section.

## QUICK TAKES

### The Bridges of Madison County (Original Broadway Cast Reunion Concert)

Performance attended: Monday, December 15, 2025 at MCC Theatre at Carnegie Hall

I was not familiar with this show, but I have of course heard of the movie, and this concert had quite a bit of buzz.

I was scheduled to see Kelli O'Hara a couple of days later

with Tom Hanks in the play, *This World of Tomorrow*, so why not get a preview of her work?

This was a rare show where the audience interrupted the show (multiple times) with standing ovations during the show. It happened both after a solo by Kelli and again after a solo by Steven Pasquale. I was not at all familiar with Steven, and I now consider myself a big fan of both of them.

Out of 14 shows during my December trip, this concert was my favorite experience. And that is saying something, because I also saw my favorite musicals *Hadestown* and *Ragtime* again (but it was my second time seeing each of those two shows on Broadway, so it is not a fair comparison). Across these three shows, many tears were shed! Now I am wondering if *The Bridges of Madison County* will get a Broadway revival, as it seems like it has aged well and is just so good. The entire original cast is outstanding.

## Beau the Musical

Performance attended: Friday, December 19, 2025 at The Distillery

*Beau the Musical* was one of the more powerful musicals I experienced in 2025. This show also has a fantastic book and music, an outstanding cast, and an intimate, immersive venue. What more can you ask for?

For much of the show, the performers were right next to me, creating a highly immersive experience. The venue was converted into a Nashville bar, and I was seated at a bar table next to the second stage.

I consider it to be an all-time favorite I would happily see again and again.

## Little Shop of Horrors

Performance attended: Sunday, December 14, 2025 at Westside Theatre/Upstairs

*Little Shop of Horrors* had been on my bucket list for a while, as so many people refer to it as their favorite show. Finally seeing it at the charming Westside Theatre in December was a bonus, as this theatre was all decorated with holiday decorations.

This was my third time seeing Andrew Durand (*Shucked, Bat Boy*), and I was not prepared for just how many characters he played in the show! He was fantastic, as was this entire cast. If you enjoy being in the splash zone, do sit in the front row. I was frightened at the end of the show (I was dead center front row), and oh it was so fun. It is more fun to not know the spoilers, so I will not comment further on the fun that happens in the front row.

## Two Strangers (Carry A Cake Across New York)

Performance attended: Friday, December 19, 2025 at Longacre Theatre

This new musical has a touching yet fun story with great original music and solid acting. I very much enjoyed the performances by Christiani Pitts and Sam Tutty.

One surprise with the show was that it was a bit more PG-13 than I expected (I assumed it would be as wholesome as *Maybe Happy Ending*), so do check the content warnings before taking young kids. For adults, the PG-13 humor adds to the entertainment.

This is another show where I enjoy listening to the cast recording, and I do so regularly. If you follow me on Instagram, you know that the song "New York" from this show is frequently my post's song. It can't always be "Empire State of Mind" when posting about New York, right?

## Gruesome Playground Injuries

Performance attended: Friday, December 19, 2025 at Lucille Lortel Theatre

I confess I primarily went to see this show to see Kara Young again, as I enjoyed her performance in *Purpose* so much. But not only did I get to experience Kara's incredible acting again, but I also got to discover Nicholas Braun's stage acting skills.

A creative choice in this show was we got to see Kara and Nicholas do their numerous wardrobe changes on stage. Watching them change while upbeat music played kept us entertained when we may have otherwise gotten bored waiting for the next scene.

I was anxious about sitting in the front row after hearing so many people say that some people won't be able to handle the gruesome stage makeup in this show, but I decided I could just look away if I needed to. I felt like people exaggerated, as the gruesome and graphic injuries tended to make me laugh at how overly graphic they were; I thankfully did not vomit or faint. As I write this, I am smiling just thinking about some of the over-the-top makeup, as it was indeed gruesome (and fun). The physical injuries were of course also a metaphor for so many emotional injuries.

I would love to see this play again, or perhaps I will just read the script, as I feel like this play is deeper than you can pick up just in a single viewing of the play, especially given the visuals which sometimes steal the show for a moment.

One thing is for sure after seeing *Purpose* and *Gruesome Playground Injuries* in 2025: I will prioritize going to see any show Kara is in.

## This World of Tomorrow

Performance attended: Wednesday, December 17, 2025 at The Shed

*This World of Tomorrow* is a sweet romantic comedy, and the cast was excellent. Sometimes I am anxious to see a film star on stage, as the skillset is very different, but Tom Hanks came through with a polished performance. I also very much enjoyed seeing Kelli O'Hara in a play after having seen her perform in a staged concert just two days earlier in *The Bridges of Madison County* Original Broadway Cast Reunion Concert. I also loved that Tom Hanks was in attendance at the concert Monday night in order to support his scene partner.

# 4

# BONUS CONTENT

I see quite a bit of community theatre, and I had the idea, why not include a community theatre production in this book? I looked back through my list of shows I saw in 2025, and two amateur productions jumped out at me: one a community theatre production and the other a high school production!

In the case of both community theatre and high school, these are unpaid volunteer actors putting in the work for the love of the art and the friendship that happens in the process.

## COMMUNITY THEATRE

### Sondheim Tribute Revue

Performance attended: Friday, July 25, 2025 at Ovation! Performing Arts Northwest at Side Quest Stage at Rolling Bay Hall

The standout community theatre production I experienced in 2025 was Ovation! Performing Arts Northwest's *Sondheim Tribute Revue*. Ovation! Performing Arts Northwest is a nonprofit organization based on Bainbridge Island, Washington, and produces musical theatre, choir concerts, and musical revues based on a theme, for example Stephen Sondheim.

While it was of course incredible to experience top talent like Bernadette Peters and Lea Salonga performing Stephen Sondheim's music on Broadway in New York City, as I discussed earlier in the book, it was also enjoyable to watch local talent and Old Friends in Kitsap County perform Sondheim on Bainbridge Island.

A difference between Ovation's show and the prior *Sondheim's Old Friends* on Broadway was the performers singing their hearts out on stage on Bainbridge Island were doing so as volunteers and for the pure joy and passion they have for the music. I saw performances on Bainbridge that brought just as much passion and emotion as did the big stars on Broadway.

In comparing the two programs, there was more overlap in songs than I remembered. This made sense, since the Broadway show was nearly three hours long and covered so many shows. The Ovation show was a bit over two hours long and also included fascinating facts about Stephen Sondheim and his songs and shows. Ovation did a really nice job organizing the order of the songs and performers; the show flowed very nicely.

Out of all of the songs that occurred in both shows, there were two I want to call out. First is "Losing My Mind," which was performed by Bernadette Peters on Broadway, and on Bainbridge, it was performed by Barbi-Jo Smith to close out Act 1. Barbi-Jo's performance was a standout performance of the evening and such a great way to close Act 1. I absolutely loved Barbi-Jo's energy and presence during this performance.

Kendra Truett had a standout performance with "The Worst Pies in London," which was sung earlier in 2025 on Broadway by Lea Salonga. I see no reason why Kendra could not be the one on that Broadway stage. Her performances were outstanding.

Matt Alder, Christy Alligood, Lee Gunby, Diane Hoeft, Margaret Johnston, Tina Kirkpatrick, Wendy LaVoy, Mallory McCollum, Misty Munro, Angela Reyes, Beau Ross, Kestrel Rundle, Vicente Velasco, and Don Warkentin also did Sondheim proud with their excellent performances. Wendi Olinger was fantastic as music director, as usual, and Avery Wong was excellent on keys. Margaret Johnston produced and directed the show, and Wendy LaVoy co-produced.

I also loved the small, intimate venue, where microphones were not needed. The piano was at just the right volume, and the sound quality was excellent.

## HIGH SCHOOL THEATRE

### Grease

Performance attended: Friday, May 9, 2025 at Bainbridge High School (Bainbridge Island, Washington)

Last but not least, I am throwing in a high school musical in this book. Why? First, it's really important to support art in schools, and if this inclusion motivates you to go see a production at your local high school, then it was worth it to add more pages.

Second, I am being completely honest when I say *Grease* at Bainbridge High School was one of my favorite shows of the year—out of over 80 shows, mostly in New York City. I am not sure it really mattered what the show was, so this praise is all about the cast and creative team more so than the book and music. Whether or not *Grease* has aged well is a topic for a different book.

I sometimes talk about the excitement of seeing an understudy make their Broadway debut, but what about the excitement of a high school student hitting that hard note in front of an audience? "Mom, I hit that note!" you might hear after the show. What's better than seeing a theatre kid feel proud for all that hard work?

I will admit school musicals can be hit or miss, but experiencing even one per year with so much joy is worth it. This show was back in May, and yet some of us still talk about how fun it was almost a year later.

As far as non-perfect production quality, I compare it to the excitement of high school sports and college sports. There will just be more mistakes made in a high school game than in a college game, and college athletes will make more mistakes than professional athletes. Similarly, high school productions will have technical issues (as do Broadway shows sometimes). But the heart and the personal growth happening on stage (and in rehearsal) might be the best in high school theatre.

I am not going to highlight any actors or name any names, since many of the cast members were minors, but this cast and creative team should be very proud of themselves, and they can now say they were possibly the only high school production in America called out in a published book focused on the best shows of 2025 on Broadway in New York City.

So yes, *Grease* at Bainbridge High School in 2025 was one of my favorite theatre experiences of the year, causing it to make this book, alongside *Hadestown, Ragtime,* Tom Hanks, Hugh Jackman, Chloë Grace Moretz, Kara Young, and more. Well done. Good job, and congrats to those involved!

Please commit to going to a high school theatre production sometime in the next year, so I don't feel silly including a high school show alongside professional Broadway shows. And remember to cheer loudly. If this inclusion motivates even one of you to attend a high school play or musical, or if it makes even one member of the *Grease* cast or creative team smile, then this was a worthwhile way to wrap up this book.

# 5
# STAGE DOOR

Thank you for reading this far! This book is an experiment to see if it should become an annual series.

If you enjoyed this book, please consider leaving a review and telling your friends about the book on social media.

You can turn your phone back on now.

# ABOUT THE AUTHOR

Brian Guy is an Off-Broadway co-producer, author, and theatre enthusiast. His books include *Broadway for Beginners: A Tourist's Guide to Broadway and Off-Broadway in New York City.*

Brian is co-founder of Neurodiversity Allies, a nonprofit organization advocating for sensory accessibility in theatre.

He is passionate about helping new and occasional theatregoers feel confident, informed, and welcome. Brian resides on Bainbridge Island in Washington State.

instagram.com/brianguytheatre
facebook.com/brianguytheatre

# ALSO BY BRIAN GUY

Broadway for Beginners: A Tourist's Guide to Broadway and Off-Broadway in New York City

# PREVIEW NIGHT PRESS

An imprint of Preview Night, LLC

previewnightpress.com

www.ingramcontent.com/pod-product-compliance
Lightning Source LLC
LaVergne TN
LVHW041538070526
838199LV00046B/1725